PAISLEY
AND THE PROVOS

Brian Rowan was born in Belfast in 1958 and is the BBC's security editor in Northern Ireland. He now lives just outside the city and is married with three children. In the IPR Press and Media awards, he has been named specialist journalist of the year, and has twice won the e-journalist category for his writing for BBC News Online. Rowan has covered the "war" and "peace" of Northern Ireland since 1989 and has been described by the award-winning author Peter Taylor as "the real insider who knows all the main players".

This is Rowan's third book since the ceasefires of 1994.

PAISLEY
AND THE PROVOS

BRIAN ROWAN

THE BREHON PRESS
BELFAST

First published 2005 by The Brehon Press Ltd
1A Bryson Street, Belfast BT5 4ES
Northern Ireland

ISBN: 1 905474 04 0

Design: December Publications
Printed by J H Haynes & Co Ltd

CONTENTS

For Margaret and Mike

ACKNOWLEDGEMENTS

This book is about a period in the life of Northern Ireland, or the North, when the politically unthinkable almost became the politically done. For many years we have watched the politics of war and peace – watched people die, watched peace arrive on our doorsteps and watched it ebb and flow. The future of this place is now in the hands of Paisley and the "Provos" and the route to a new government here is business for the Democratic Unionist Party and Sinn Féin to deal with. They are the new main players in our politics – the makers of the future.

I wanted to write this book – and to write it quickly – for a number of reasons. It was best done when detail and developments were fresh in the mind. It is set in the period of the DUP and Sinn Féin taking the lead political roles here. It tells the story of how close they came to doing a deal in 2004, how far away they were from it in the end, and then the falling down and the picking up of the pieces of this peace process. The IRA has now ordered an end to its armed campaign and decommissioned its weapons. The British Army has responded with a massive scaling down of its operations, and political minds are again focused on resuming negotiations designed to make "the deal of all deals".

This book is about trying to record all of the above, to set out one journalist's thinking and reporting on what has been arguably the most important phase of this peace process, a phase in which the unthinkable has become the possible and then the probable. I couldn't have done it without the help of many others. I want to thank Ian Paisley, Martin McGuinness, Peter Robinson, General John de Chastelain, the Rev Harold Good, Sir Hugh Orde, David Ervine, Jackie McDonald and all the others for their contributions to the telling of this two-year story.

I also want to thank the sources who cannot be named, but who will recognise their contributions in the pages and the words that follow.

My colleagues at the BBC in Belfast have given me tremendous support over many years, and I particularly want to thank Andrew Colman, Mervyn Jess, Seamus Kelters, Neal Sutherland and Damien Magee.   Others will find their names scattered throughout this book. Outside the BBC, David McKittrick, Eamonn Mallie and Deric Henderson have been great and trusted friends. In my journalistic career I'm moving on now, but it has been a great honour to have been entrusted with the job I've done for many years in our war and peace. I want to say thank you to all those who made that possible.

Jim McDowell sent me on my way and many others have helped along the road: Robin Walsh, Keith Baker, John Conway, Paul Robinson, Eddie Fleming, Tom Kelly, Pat Loughrey, Tony Maddox, Tim Cooke, Michael Cairns, Kathleen and Anna Carragher, Angelina Fusco and Peter Taylor to mention but a few. I have a family that is second to none when it comes to giving support. The Hursons – my cousins Marie Therese and Ciaran – made a huge contribution to the book. Marie Therese is the photographer for *Paisley and the Provos* and Ciaran designed the cover. Their work speaks for itself.

My wife Val and my "kids" Ruairi, Elle and PJ have held me up and given me all the support I've needed in covering this war and peace. It's now my turn to give them all the support they need.

I also want to thank my parents, Margaret and Mike, and the Braniff girls – Lily, Rose, Veronica, Teresa, Kathleen and Frances – and my "older" cousin Mary for keeping us on our toes and keeping us right at all times and in all places. There are two others to thank and they will know why. They are the two Daves – Mills and Malcolm – one who can't tell the difference between a £20 and a £10 note, and the other who has a great story to tell about "the lion and the penguin". So, read the book. Shout and scream and yell and laugh. Remember what we've been through and think about where we are going.

Brian Rowan
November 2005

PROLOGUE

FIRST WORDS

"The Provisional movement is a broad church...You have everything from people on a political wing who never served militarily, through (to) military doves now, who appreciated that the best that they were going to get in the war with us was a draw. We realised that too; thoughtful police officers and soldiers realised it as well...We are all going to have our little victories against each other, but, bluntly, you couldn't go on with a life of Loughgalls one day, and Airey Neaves and Mountbatten the next day. That's the crazy thing...You've people who believe that there was a possible military victory...and, actually on extreme wings, you have people there who would be quite indistinguishable in their outlook from the dissident republicans...even if we are the last ones standing, we will never compromise." *Senior intelligence officer, October 2005, describing the IRA organisation as it debated its future.*

"What would happen, say that I went into government, and the IRA did something again...(it would be said) 'you were a fool', and all that you did would be forgotten in five minutes. You're actually putting your future into the hands of the IRA. Well, it's like asking me to put my soul into the hands of the devil, and I can only describe it that way... Any politician that's in the position I'm in, he must realise that if he's going to take decisions, which he'll have to take, he must be satisfied in his own mind; and if I was satisfied in my own mind about things, I would have the courage to do it." *DUP leader Ian Paisley, October 2005, on the prospects of the DUP and Sinn Féin being in government together.*

"As someone who is quite used to shocks of all descriptions it was a bit of a tremor to say the least, that we had an almost flip-flop situation by Tony Blair from expressing his view that Paisley wasn't prepared to do a deal in the immediate aftermath of the (November 2003 Assembly) elections, to early in 2004 beginning to give us a very strong message, that strengthened of course during the course of the year, that Paisley was up for a deal. And, so, we were very keenly interested in that, and argued the whole way through that if this was the case, obviously the logical thing for Ian Paisley to do was to sit down with the Sinn Féin leadership and to talk to us face to face, both himself and Peter Robinson." *Sinn Féin chief negotiator Martin McGuinness, October 2005, on the possibility of a deal with the DUP.*

"Suddenly they realised that all of what they (republicans had) talked about, they might actually have to do, and Paisley was up for it (a deal), and I think there was a desperate search around for an exit at this stage; not so much, and maybe it's guesswork at this stage, I'm not convinced it's because they didn't want to do a deal, as they didn't feel they could do a deal at that stage. They hadn't prepared their organisation for the steps that had to be taken...So, I think at that stage they recognised that Ian Paisley was for real...and, in looking for an excuse, they jumped upon a speech that he made in Ballymena – a speech which I think should have been perhaps looked at in more theological terms than political terms." *DUP deputy leader Peter Robinson, October 2005, accusing republicans of running away from the negotiations in 2004.*

"Measure the atmosphere in the unionist community against the atmosphere in the nationalist community. And we have a nationalist community whose leadership have encouraged them to look at the hills, and a unionist community whose leadership encourage them to look at their boots. And I've often said before that all 'Prods' are clairvoyant, that it's never good news. The day that nothing happens to us should be a good day, but we see it rather as just one day closer to the day that something will happen to us." *Loyalist politician David Ervine, October 2005, commenting on the mood inside his community.*

"The problem with loyalism and the paramilitary organisations as I see it, is we're being treated as insignificant and we have been for quite some time, and now because the IRA have given up their guns, they want the loyalists to give up their guns. But if they are insignificant with the guns, what are they going to be like without them? They are going to be slapped round the head and told to go home and get into the house." *Loyalist leader Jackie McDonald, speaking in October 2005.*

Close your eyes and think of this place not that many years ago. Think of its killing fields, its war and the headstones that tell the story of three thousand deaths and more. Now, open your eyes to this new day. Has the IRA really gone away? Are its weapons now beyond use? Is the British Army about to end the longest running military operation in its history? Are Paisley and the "Provos" on the doorstep of a once unthinkable deal, or is it all too good to be true?

The political jury is still out, but there is a new reality here, a reality that places the business of deal-making in the hands of the Democratic Unionist Party (DUP) and Sinn Féin. In the new Northern Ireland – in the North – we now talk of the possibility of Ian Paisley and Martin McGuinness sharing government as First and Deputy First Ministers. Their parties are the new lead players in a peace process which began with ceasefires more than a decade ago.

But the war is not yet over. There are other guns out there: the guns of the loyalists which have been turned on each other. Here, murder is now described as "the tying up (of) a few loose ends".

So, the decommissioning General John de Chastelain has completed just part of his work. In September 2005, in the company of new church witnesses – Father Alex Reid and the Reverend Harold Good – he put the IRA's weapons beyond use. Two months earlier the leadership of that organisation, Oglaigh na hEireann, had ordered an end to its armed campaign. And now we wait. Gerry Adams persuaded the IRA that there was a political alternative to its armed struggle. Less than a year ago, he and Paisley almost did business but the IRA refused to wear the "sackcloth and ashes" that the "Big Man" of unionism had suggested and refused to allow the decommissioning process to be photographed.

"We were bitterly disappointed that December (2004) didn't come to a successful conclusion, but none of us were surprised." This is Martin McGuinness speaking. "We've been through all of this ground before. We know what we are dealing with. We knew what we were dealing with in David Trimble. We know what we are dealing with in Ian Paisley.

"Certainly from our point of view, we think that any serious player within the process who was, as the two Prime Ministers have said he was, determined to get an agreement which would give him some sort of political immortality in the future, wouldn't have allowed a photograph to wreck that prospect."

But Paisley's son, Ian junior, says this was about much more than a photograph. This was about testing the "sincerity" of republicans. He will tell you that his father will do the right deal and that there is something that republicans need to understand.

"He has always taken the view that if he can get a democratic settlement then the people who are entitled to be in government will then be in government… I believe, and republicans need to understand this, that the only person that they can ultimately do a deal with that will actually stick with unionism and will actually deliver unionism, is with Ian Paisley. And the sooner republicans, democratic republicans, do that deal the better."

Within weeks of that broken-down negotiation in December 2004 the IRA was linked to the biggest bank robbery in UK history and to the murder in Belfast of a Catholic man, Robert McCartney. This is a process that can make sense one day and nonsense the next. But now, there is a chance that the "deal of all deals" can be made. The intelligence assessment has the IRA in "hibernation". It has swallowed the "digestible chunks" of an end to its armed campaign and the completion of the decommissioning process, but it did not disband. It is waiting for the proof that politics can work, and we are waiting to see if Paisley really will do business with the "Provos".

CHAPTER ONE

TEA FOR TWO

"Can you take courageous initiatives which will achieve your aims by purely political and democratic activity?" Gerry Adams in a speech to the IRA, April 6, 2005.

"The leadership of Oglaigh na hEireann has formally ordered an end to the armed campaign... All IRA units have been ordered to dump arms." IRA response to Adams, July 28, 2005.

"I honestly do feel that if they (the IRA) had disbanded, and taken that next step along, there would have been a serious bit of walking." Senior intelligence officer, October 2005, commenting on the outcome of IRA debate.

"That's the IRA out of the equation – no question or doubt about it whatsoever. And I have stated ... that I believed that the IRA would keep their commitments, and they have done so now very spectacularly by putting their weapons beyond use, under the tutelage of General de Chastelain, in the company of a Finnish General, a United States diplomat, a Protestant clergyman and a Catholic priest." Martin McGuinness, October 2005, commenting on the IRA's July statement and subsequent decommissioning.

JULY 23, 2005. It was the conversation that convinced me that the IRA statement was now imminent. I was in west Belfast – in the constituency of the Sinn Féin President Gerry Adams – sitting across the table from a long-time republican contact. He had been doing his shopping and we had agreed to meet in the supermarket café just before noon. We had tea for two, a scone and some Veda bread and one of those conversations in which you hear more in the silence than you do in the words. The negotiations that were going on in the background were at a crucial stage, both in terms of the talking inside the IRA and between Sinn Féin and the British and Irish governments. But I heard enough – or interpreted enough – to understand what I was being told and, within an hour, I was broadcasting on *BBC Radio Ulster* the possibility of "a significant development within days". On air, I posed the question: Could that mean that we get that statement from the IRA? And I answered: Yes we could.

"Unless the Brits fuck this up in the next couple of days, my personal view is it's coming this week," my source had told me.

He was in a position to know, and I was confident that his guidance could be relied upon. But that "fuck up" that he feared nearly came in Dublin, where an argument over the precise details of how decommissioning would occur was taken right down to the wire.

The statement we were waiting for was the IRA's response to a speech by Adams in Belfast in April, a speech he delivered at Conway Mill – the same place he had used to speak directly to a republican audience just hours before the first act of IRA decommissioning in October 2001. This time, the Sinn Féin President was asking for much more. His speech was billed as "an address to the IRA".

And here, on the Falls Road, he was using his words to talk to "the men and women of Oglaigh na hEireann, the volunteer soldiers of the Irish Republican Army", and he was asking them to accept an alternative to "armed struggle".

This was Adams urging the IRA to end its decades-long campaign and to go quietly from the battlefield. That was the historical significance of this moment, and the Sinn Féin

President spoke with Martin McGuinness at his shoulder. The two men who had pointed the IRA in the direction of ceasefires and decommissioning, and who had achieved those things by keeping the organisation largely intact, were now looking towards another phase in the peace process.

This would be a phase without an armed IRA, a phase that would see sweeping changes to the security landscape of Northern Ireland and a phase which would once again open up the potential for some sort of political arrangement between Ian Paisley's Democratic Unionist Party and the "Provos". What was once the unthinkable could now be seen in the wider frame beyond Conway Mill, beyond the Falls Road and beyond the words of this Adams speech. The republican leaders of 2005 were now moving the IRA into the final phase of its "Long War".

Before they were spoken, the words of this Adams speech would have been known to only a very small group of republicans – those within the Sinn Féin "core group". Inside that negotiating team Ted Howell, Aidan McAteer, Leo Green, Séanna Walsh and Richard McAuley work alongside Adams, McGuinness and Gerry Kelly. The latest speech they had prepared was now about to be heard by many more across the Republican movement – inside the IRA and inside Sinn Féin. The Army Council knew what Adams was about to say. This was not the Sinn Féin President manoeuvring as part of some complex deal-making process with the governments and the unionists.

What we were seeing and hearing was something different. This was a unilateral republican initiative designed to take the IRA and its guns off the agenda before the next round of political talks. Late on Tuesday April 5 – on the eve of the Conway Mill speech – Richard McAuley called me at home. He would have known every word that Adams was about to speak, the internal and external significance of the speech and how and why it had come to fruition. He told me there would be a "keynote" address the following day – a speech in which Adams would map out the "necessary next steps" for republicans if the peace process was to succeed. Hours earlier, Tony Blair had announced that elections would be held on May 5, and in Northern Ireland those would be in the 18 parliamentary constituencies and in the 26 local council areas. While republicans would argue that the timing was coincidental, others – particular unionists – saw the Adams speech as an election stunt and as an attempt at damage limitation after the Northern Bank robbery and the murder of Belfast man Robert McCartney.

Downing Street and the Northern Ireland Office knew that the Adams speech was coming. Indeed, they knew much more than that. They had an advance copy of the text and they recognised the potential in these latest republican words. But they also knew that it would only be possible to assess the political worth of all of this when the IRA responded. Tom Kelly – Blair's Downing Street spokesman and my news editor at the BBC in Belfast at the time of the IRA's August '94 ceasefire – made that clear.

"The key will be what the IRA does as a result (of the Adams speech), and it is on that that any final judgement will be made."

Years earlier, Kelly had heard me describe that '94 ceasefire as the political equivalent of the cow actually jumping over the moon. I did so because it ran against the republican grain. The "Brits" were still in, not out, Ireland was still divided, not united, and, at that time, any talk of an accommodation between republicans, the British and the unionists would have been dismissed in a sentence including the words pie and sky. In the ups and downs of the peace process, Kelly and I have had many conversations since about the cow and the moon, and it was something we would return to within minutes of the IRA's response to Adams.

It was clear in the April speech what the Sinn Féin President was asking the IRA to do. This was about relinquishing the republican throne, it was about the IRA taking a back seat, it was about the organisation doing so publicly and convincingly, it was about the IRA saying it had confidence in the Adams peace strategy, and, more than anything else, it was about the IRA ending its armed struggle. However it chose to do that, it had to be said in language that was easily understood. This time, there could be no interpretation through the aid of a conflict resolution dictionary. In his April speech, Adams spoke in plain language.

"In the past I have defended the right of the IRA to engage in armed struggle," he said.

"I did so because there was no alternative for those who would not bend the knee, or turn a blind eye to oppression, or for those who wanted a national republic. Now there is an alternative... The way forward is by building political support for republican and democratic objectives across Ireland and by winning support for those goals internationally. I want to use this occasion therefore to appeal to the leadership of Oglaigh na hEireann to fully embrace and accept this alternative. Can you take courageous initiatives which will achieve your aims by purely political and democratic activity?"

That was the big question to the IRA – that final sentence in which Adams asked it to definitively end the long republican "war", to put its faith in a political alternative, to put its faith in him and McGuinness and those around them. There was a huge difference between the ceasefire the IRA had been observing and what was now being asked for. The Adams speech was looking beyond the "complete cessation of military operations" first declared in August 1994 and then restored in July 1997. This was the stuff of endgame, putting down the armed struggle and picking up something else.

"That struggle can now be taken forward by other means," Adams said. "I say this with the authority of my office as President of Sinn Féin."

But would he have risked that "authority" in such a public way – in a speech carried by all the major news outlets – without first knowing the mind of the IRA leadership? The view inside the intelligence world was that Adams had done his homework.

"You've got to appreciate that Gerry Adams would not have made the statement without a really in-depth assessment that he would have carried the day," a senior intelligence officer told me.

"He knew he could control the organisation through its various structures and systems, key people in the right place... There had been so much acceptance of the various types of decommissioning, of the Provisional movement, through its political representatives, being up at the big White House at Stormont, of a variety of things like this, that (he knew) they clearly could carry the day with the vast majority of members, volunteers."

Despite their constant denials, the security and political assessments still placed Adams and McGuinness on the Army Council of the IRA, and, within days, that leadership had given orders for the debate to begin.

Adams had accepted that there was the need for "intense internal consultation", and he had asked that this be initiated as quickly as possible. The IRA would respond on July 28 – 113 days after the Adams speech of April 6.

"Obviously an awful lot of thought went into what would go into Gerry's speech." This is Martin McGuinness speaking to me.

McGUINNESS: We were very determined to bring about a circumstance whereby the way in which the IRA were being used persistently as an excuse to block progress, we were clearly of the view that that should be removed from the unionists and from Michael McDowell (Irish Justice Minister) and from others. So, Gerry's speech obviously sparked a debate within the IRA. There's no doubt that it was a serious discussion all over the country with many different views expressed.

ROWAN: Was it a debate, or was it a briefing or was it a consultation, was it people being told or was it people being asked, in your opinion?

McGUINNESS: It was more people being told, well this is the situation at the moment, these are the political circumstances that exist, have a discussion about that, give us your views. It was certainly not people being told, from the information that I have, this is what we are going to do, what do you think of it? And that's what made it, I think, a much more valuable debate. Some people, I think, did argue at the beginning that what the IRA leadership should do is go to the volunteers and say, well this is it, this is the way that we are going to do it. My information is that the IRA approached it in a completely different way. They went along to people and outlined the political circumstances that existed and asked them to have a debate.

ROWAN: But at the end of the day, the leadership has to decide.

McGUINNESS: And they did decide then on the back of the views that were expressed from their units and their volunteers all over the island of Ireland, and, of course, in taking the decisions that they've taken they have absolutely changed the ball game for everyone, and I think that there is no doubt whatsoever that the speech made by Gerry Adams in April and the IRA response to that clearly shows that the IRA, big time, have bought into Gerry Adams' analysis of where things need to go, have bought into his view that the best way forward for Irish republicanism is by prosecuting the struggle, and the struggle isn't over, but by purely peaceful and democratic means, and I see that as a huge vindication of Gerry Adams' leadership.

In between the Adams speech and the IRA's response, the elections had been good to Sinn Féin, but maybe not as good as the party had expected – not as good as the canvassing had suggested. Four MPs became five with Conor Murphy taking the Newry and Armagh seat to join Adams, McGuinness, Pat Doherty and Michelle Gildernew. Across the counts, the gap between Sinn Féin and its rival for the nationalist vote, the SDLP, was close to fifty thousand votes, but the party once led by John Hume still won three seats. Its new leader Mark Durkan succeeded Hume as MP in the Foyle constituency with a comfortable victory over his Sinn Féin rival Mitchel McLaughlin. The sitting MP Eddie McGrady had an equally convincing win over Catriona Ruane in South Down, and Alasdair McDonnell was a surprise winner in South Belfast, benefiting from a split unionist vote. In the council elections, Sinn Féin added 18 seats to its previous total, now 126, while the SDLP dropped 16 to 101.

In the post-election analysis, there was a privately expressed opinion within republicanism that while the bank job had not cost Sinn Féin votes, the McCartney murder had. The party lost its seat in the Pottinger ward, where Robert McCartney had lived, and Sinn Féin's tally of seats across the councils was probably something in the region of twenty below what had been anticipated. But the real story of these elections was one of DUP domination on the unionist side. Paisley's party took nine Westminster and 182 council seats. In the General Election, Sylvia Hermon was the only Ulster Unionist survivor. David Trimble lost his seat in Upper Bann and, within days, resigned as party leader. He was succeeded by Sir Reg Empey – a former minister in the power-sharing Executive. In the election, the Ulster Unionist Party (UUP) had been trounced, and any future political deal-making would be for Paisley and Adams to work out with the governments. The new political reality of November '03 had been confirmed in this latest electoral test.

Throughout that period of the elections and beyond, the IRA was talking to itself in that internal debate on its future. It was a discussion from the top to the bottom of the organisation – structured in the shape of small gatherings. IRA "volunteers" were given a meeting point and then taken to undisclosed venues. There was tight security around the meetings. No "gadgetry" was allowed, mobile phones, etc. At each of the meetings there was a "recognised, senior middle-management figure" from the IRA leadership. An IRA summary of progress since the ceasefires was read. In the discussions, the leadership figure did not offer an opinion on the question of the future of the IRA. The debate was noted, and no time constraints were placed on the discussions. Some of the meetings ran from early morning to late at night. It was an IRA debate. This was the republican "Army" deciding its future. To quote one source, it was "a military discussion in a political context".

That source described the debate as "democratic", and said that in the way it was constructed, the "fingerprints of every IRA member" would be on the outcome. That said there would be no IRA vote on the final leadership decision. There would not be what the organisation calls a General Army Convention at which that leadership would have to stand for re-election and where delegates from across the IRA would debate and then decide future strategy. Democracy meant the membership was consulted and briefed, the mood assessed and then there was a statement from the "army" leadership to its volunteers – a statement detailing the orders from the Army Council.

The police were monitoring developments and the chief constable Sir Hugh Orde was satisfied there would be no split. In an interview for this book, he told me that, going into this debate, the republican leadership would have known that it was going to take the bulk of its organisation with it. He would have been fully aware of that intelligence assessment I outlined earlier.

"I would be amazed if that when they said what they said, they did not have the confidence that they were going to carry most of their people with them… They're good at this… I was fairly clear that we were not going to get some mass exodus to dissidents – that, much on the grounds, that dissidents are pretty useless, and disrupted, and under arrest North and South, and we are continuing to arrest them. So, if I'm someone who has some sort of belief that I fought for an organisation that was a worthy cause, in their perception, am I going to join something that lacks credibility, has no political dimension to it really, and (is) just a bunch of serial killers who can't move on? Maybe I'm not... You may have some grumpy people, but the likelihood is the grumpy people will just walk away," Orde said.

The IRA meetings and discussions which were held threw up the type of issues you would expect. Decommissioning was discussed. There were questions about the loyalists – about how vulnerable nationalist areas would be protected. The issue of IRA disbandment was not discussed, but every other possible outcome was – up to and including what the IRA leadership eventually ordered, an end to its armed campaign. I am told it took a while for the discussions to arrive at that point. There was some criticism of the Adams strategy – or the Sinn Féin peace strategy – that it wasn't working or hadn't delivered. Matters relating to the IRA constitution were raised, but these were dealt with separately. It is an illegal document and copies were not available at these meetings. The consequences of a possible police raid had been considered. There were weeks and weeks of secret discussions, all logged and taken back to the leadership. And, before the IRA spoke publicly, all of its members would be brought back to similar meetings and told of the decision of the Army Council. This was about 24 hours before all of this played out in the public arena of the peace process.

"The IRA and the Provisional Movement have been quite good at managing change in digestible chunks." This is a senior intelligence officer speaking to me in an interview for this book, which I recorded on October 11 2005.

"You can't do everything at once... If you don't bring your volunteers with you, you end up with splits, and sort of mutinies and rebellions... Adams' statement wasn't going to lose anybody. The reply was, potentially... I honestly do feel that if they had disbanded and taken that next step along, there would have been a serious bit of walking...

"Going into hibernation for three years, or two or three years, cutting out their activities, and then talking about making themselves into some Irish equivalent of the British Legion or something like that, might be more digestible. Much as I think that it's important that all paramilitary organisations are disbanded and stood down, I think if they had disbanded, a significant minority of key people would have walked."

As the IRA debate began, one republican sketched out a possible outcome. This was at a meeting on Friday April 8. We were chewing the fat, thinking out loud about the logical outworking of the Adams initiative. He knew what Adams wanted and, if things went to plan, he expected that the arms issue – decommissioning – would be dealt with before the next political negotiations. Church witnesses could be involved, but there would be no photographs. Paisley had demanded these in the negotiations that took place in late 2004. The IRA would not disband. There were no plans for an IRA Convention (such a meeting is required for the organisation's leadership to "conclude a final peace"), but the source suggested there could be "a significant period of quiet" before the next political negotiations. The next report by the Independent Monitoring Commission – a kind of ceasefire watchdog – was due in October, followed by another in January 2006, and the hope of the governments was that these would set the mood for new talks. The assessment given to me in that meeting of April 8 worked its way into the IRA response of July 28. Adams would get his way.

That response from the IRA took a little longer than expected, not because a problem had emerged within the internal debate, but because of unexpected happenings. Here in Northern Ireland, eleven and more years after the ceasefires of 1994, there are incidents that will never be forgotten and individuals who will never be forgiven.

The Shankill bomb of 1993 is one such incident and Sean Kelly is one such individual. He is one of the "bogey men" of the

Northern Ireland "Troubles". I was on the Shankill Road that Saturday in October 1993, not long after the explosion, and I felt the rage around me. Sean Kelly had been there earlier – there as part of an IRA "active service unit" on an apparent mission to kill the loyalist leader Johnny Adair and his paramilitary associates. But Adair and his men were not in the UDA office above the fish shop that day and they escaped the IRA bomb. Innocent civilians were slaughtered – men, women and children – and one of Kelly's associates, Thomas Begley, also died in the blast. Long after that day, I interviewed one of the police officers who was first on the scene. He remembered everything, digging in the rubble, finding a child's shoe and not wanting to dig anymore. He knew what he was about to find. And that is why the Shankill and Sean Kelly are etched into peoples' memories. It is why, as this place inches forward, there will always be people who will look back.

I was also in the car park of the Maze Prison in July 2000 as Sean Kelly was released from jail – freed early as part of the Good Friday Agreement, freed just seven years after the Shankill bomb. I have met him, or bumped into him I should say, several times since in north Belfast, usually at times of tension on the so-called interfaces where the Protestant and Catholic communities live cheek by jowl. You would see him in the company of senior republicans such as Gerry Kelly, Brendan McFarlane and Eddie Copeland. One night, I watched as he intervened to stop teenagers from throwing petrol bombs. And, in republican eyes, Kelly was just that – a calming influence in these situations – but others saw him differently, saw him as that "bogey man" and saw him as the bomber. Senior figures in the DUP wanted him back in jail, and among those pressing the government to do that was the MP Jeffrey Donaldson.

"It was clear to us that Kelly had been engaged in terrorist-related activities over a significant period of time," Donaldson told me in a conversation for this book. "Not only had he been at the forefront in riotous situations in the Ardoyne area, but we are

also informed by security sources that he was the local
commander, or held a position of command, in that area. In this
capacity, we believe he had ordered a number of punishment
attacks including shootings."

On June 15, two months or so into the IRA debate, the new
Northern Ireland Secretary of State, Peter Hain – Paul Murphy's
successor at Hillsborough after the May elections – suspended
Kelly's early release licence. He was arrested and returned to jail
three days later. Hain said he was acting on security information
that Kelly had become re-involved in terrorism. No other detail
was given, but in non-attributable conversations with police and
political sources, I had heard this suggestion of Kelly's
involvement in punishment attacks. According to a senior DUP
source, Hain disclosed this information when he met party
members at Stormont days after Kelly's arrest.

"When we met with the Secretary of State after he had taken
the decision to have Kelly returned to prison, he confirmed that
the evidence and intelligence information in his possession about
Kelly's activities was significant," Jeffrey Donaldson told me.

This is not how republicans viewed things. In their eyes this
was Hain acquiescing to unionist demands. It was the so-called
"securocrats" at their work.

As far as republicans were concerned, there was no significant
evidence or intelligence information, and, then, there was the
timing of the arrest. Why now? Why five years after his release?
Why at such a delicate and sensitive moment in this process? As
the IRA debate continued, there was now a problem. Kelly is not
a senior figure in that organisation. He would not have been one
of the key, influential voices in that internal discussion. But, as far
as republicans were concerned, he was one of theirs, and one of
theirs was being held as a political hostage. It was not said out
loud, but while Kelly was in jail there would be no IRA statement.

It was said quietly to me in that conversation in the
supermarket café on Saturday July 23 – but said to me in a way

that suggested that this was going to be, or had already been, "sorted". To quote one source, the "Brits" were going to have to take "a self-inflicted hit". That said, that "hit" would depend on the quality and the clarity of the IRA statement. Hain would have to be convinced before taking the final decision on Kelly's release. So, at a private meeting in the Lady Grey room at Hillsborough Castle on the afternoon of Wednesday July 27, Gerry Adams gave copies of the statement to the Secretary of State and to the political director at the Northern Ireland Office, Jonathan Phillips; but the Sinn Féin President wanted them back. It meant that Phillips had to copy it down in long hand, and, later, it was faxed to Downing Street. The words of "P O'Neill" were now in the British political system. Speaking to me for this book, Hain said that as he read through the text, on that Wednesday afternoon, "it was very evident... that this was something dramatic, with the promise of it being, in Martin McGuinness's words, momentous". The Secretary of State sensed that this was "one of those kinds of moments in history".

He was struck by the fact that the statement was "unconditional". The words were ordering an end to the armed campaign, and Hain felt he had just been given "the most significant statement ever" from the IRA. The Secretary of State was not surprised; he believed from his talks with Adams and McGuinness "that they really were determined to deliver something that was intended to be a final statement". All of this was on the eve of that organisation's public announcement as its "volunteers" were still being told of the Army Council's decision.

Inside the IRA, this initiative was being described as "unilateral". It was that in terms of the IRA having to go first, speak first and clearly about its intentions. But Adams and McGuinness and those in Sinn Féin's "core group" – the political negotiating team – and in the IRA leadership would have known by now what was going to flow from the statement. This is a process that has always moved in a two-way street. What one side does has to be matched by the other. Adams and McGuinness had been to Downing Street on Monday, July 25 and, later that day, had met the Irish Taoiseach, Bertie Ahern. In these meetings, Blair and Ahern would have heard a detailed account of what the IRA was prepared to say and do, but, even at this late stage, they were not given the final IRA text. That would have to wait for the Adams-Hain meeting on Wednesday.

Late on Tuesday, July 26, Blair's spokesman Tom Kelly had told me: "We haven't seen the final text (and), until we actually see it, we reserve judgement."

I sensed that Kelly's instinct was that things were going to be OK, indeed better than that. But we were now in that edgy, nervous endgame as far as this particular negotiation was concerned and, in Downing Street, they were not counting their political chickens before they hatched.

The final judgements that had to be made spanned a number of issues – not just the release of Sean Kelly, but the political responses at prime ministerial level both in London and Dublin and, if the IRA was leaving the stage, there was the matter of the British military response.

That would be how the gap would be filled between what the IRA said and did and the next phase of political talking, which would have as its objective some deal or working arrangement between Paisley's party and the "Provos".

By shortly after seven o'clock on Saturday evening, July 23, just hours after that meeting in the supermarket café, I had spoken to Sean Kelly's solicitor, Kevin Winters. He was in Donegal and we agreed to chat again on Monday. But, in this initial conversation, he told me that plans for an application for a judicial review of the case had been put on ice.

Instead, he was expecting to make an application to the Sentence Review Commission – established as part of the Good Friday Agreement to process the prisoner applications for early release. It is also the body that adjudicates in cases like this when a prisoner's licence has been suspended by the Secretary of State. Winters was seeking specific information from the police, the Northern Ireland Office and others before making that application, and, over the next few days, we would stay in touch. We chatted several times on Wednesday July 27, and it was just before nine o'clock that evening that he called me with the news of Kelly's release. His client had been freed just minutes earlier.

It was a day of some urgency – a day of many conversations involving a whole range of people in many different places. Republicans wanted Sean Kelly out that evening before the prison was locked down for the night. This was not something that could wait until the following morning. So, on the evening of July 27 – after that Hillsborough meeting involving Adams and Hain – Jonathan Phillips contacted the Director General of the Prison Service Robin Maysfield. This was to confirm a direction from the Secretary of State for Kelly to be freed on temporary release under prison rule 27. Both the NIO and Maysfield spoke to Sinn Féin's Gerry Kelly, who was dealing with this matter. Inside Maghaberry Jail, on landing four in Roe House – which is the segregated republican wing – Sean Kelly was told to pack his bags. He was then escorted by a prison officer to a reception area, where Maysfield told him that he was being discharged on temporary release. The presence of the Director General of the Prison Service was an indication of the importance of this issue. This was now in the hour between eight and nine, and Kelly was then taken in a prison van to the Quaker's car park at the jail, where he was met by Gerry Kelly, Sinn Féin party councillor Caral Ni Chuilin and another republican, John O'Hagan. He knows Maghaberry Prison – knows it from the inside. It was where he was held after being arrested in March 2002 as part of the police investigation into the break-in at Special Branch offices at Castlereagh. No one has been brought before the courts in connection with that robbery, but O'Hagan faced other intelligence-gathering charges. He was freed in September 2004, and with others had helped organise the campaign to highlight Sean Kelly's arrest and to press for his release.

At the jail, on this the eve of the IRA's announcement, the four republicans posed for a photograph that would be published in the following day's edition of *An Phoblacht*. In all that was happening during that evening of July 27, the Sentence Review Commission was in the dark. Kelly had been freed on "temporary release" on the instructions of Hain, and, the following morning, Kevin Winters would make a formal application for a review of the case. My colleague Gareth Gordon, the BBC's political correspondent, had also been contacted by a unionist source and told that Kelly had been freed. The news was leaking from the jail, but the Winters conversation gave me the context of the release and set out the next steps.

Within a few minutes, I had dictated a couple of sentences to my colleague Ian McTear on the radio news desk in Belfast and, at nine o'clock, the BBC broke the story that Kelly was out. This was the clearest signal that the IRA statement was now imminent.

The following morning Kelly's legal team hand delivered papers to the offices of the Sentence Review Commission in the centre of Belfast, including a statement from Sean Kelly, which I have been shown:

"...My licence was suspended by a notice of suspension issued by the Secretary of State and dated 15/6/05. The Northern Ireland Prison Service in correspondence to me on this date stated that the Secretary of State believed that on the basis of information available to him that I breached the terms of my licence and had become 're-involved in the commission, preparation or instigation of acts of terrorism connected with the affairs of Northern Ireland and become a danger to the public.' I wish to contend that I have not acted in breach of the conditions specified in the Northern Ireland (Sentences) Act 1998... I have not become and I am not likely to become concerned in the commission, preparation or instigation of acts of terrorism.

Furthermore I have not become and I am not likely to become a danger to the public.

"I am a supporter of the current peace process. Since my release from prison in 2000, I and other ex-prisoners, civic community and political representatives have worked positively within the north Belfast community particularly around interface areas."

Within days this matter was settled. On August 5 the Commission wrote to Kevin Winters. He was told a panel of commissioners had considered:

- The application of the prisoner including the statements of his witnesses;
- The response from the Prison Service on the 29 July 2005;
- The News Release from the Secretary of State dated 28 July 2005.

"In the circumstances, the Commissioners were satisfied that Mr Kelly has not broken the licence condition(s) specified in section 9 of the Act and hereby indicate that they are minded to make a substantive determination to the effect that your client's licence should be confirmed."

Kelly's arrest 48 days earlier was a very dramatic development which soon made its way into every news outlet, but now, in private correspondence, the matter was closed. A story, which had emerged in a blaze of publicity, was being allowed to disappear very quietly.

Days earlier, Hain had made his position clear. The IRA statement – that was shown to him by Adams on July 27 – had "created a new situation" and had changed the context of his original decision to suspend Kelly's licence.

"Having seen the statement I judged that it materially affected the evidence that I would have submitted to the Sentence Review Commissioners," Hain said.

The rest of us saw the statement at around lunchtime on Thursday, July 28. It was a day that had been choreographed by Sinn Féin and the IRA, but it was a day when the political dancers momentarily lost their step. Adams was in Dublin, McGuinness in Washington and Pat Doherty in London and all would speak at late afternoon news conferences. Publication of the weekly republican newspaper *An Phoblacht* was delayed. It would carry the IRA statement in full along with a photograph of Sean Kelly's release, and it would be on the streets of Dublin soon after Adams' four o'clock news conference.

The drum roll for all of this would be news reports of the IRA statement at two o'clock, and, about an hour before then, the embargoed words of "P O'Neill" would be passed to a number of journalists, including myself.

This time the IRA would speak in words and pictures. As well as its statement, there would be a DVD on which the words of the leadership were read by Séanna Walsh, one of the longest serving republican prisoners and a cellmate and close friend of Bobby Sands – the first man to die during the republican hunger strike of 1981. From a republican perspective, Walsh had all the right credentials to read this statement, and in preparation for Thursday's IRA announcement, he had been filmed at an undisclosed location in Belfast 24 hours earlier. By the following morning, the statement had also been read and assessed inside the British political system. Just after ten, I received a message from one of my sources saying that things were "looking very good". The IRA text had passed its first test. The "Brits" were clearly content with what they had and that was important in terms of the next steps in this process.

By noon, the IRA's spokesman had called me on my mobile phone. We would meet within the hour and I would be accompanied by my journalist colleague Eamonn Mallie. The IRA's director of publicity – the current day "P O'Neill" – said he would see us at the same place where we had met the last time. The last time was March, when he had given us a statement in which the IRA said it had offered to shoot the killers of Robert McCartney. But there would be no more shooting from the IRA if the orders in this latest Army Council statement were obeyed. It was in the hour between noon and one on that Thursday, July 28, that choreography turned to chaos. Somehow the IRA statement made its way onto a website and then onto the airwaves of a number of stations in the Republic. The planned two o'clock embargo was now gone. Two of my editors, Andrew Colman and Michael Cairns, spoke to me on the phone.

They knew I was on my way to meet the man from the IRA. I told them the text sounded right. But it wasn't just the words that they were reading to me that convinced me of the authenticity of the statement. It was the accompanying explanatory note that Séanna Walsh had been asked to read the statement by the leadership of Oglaigh na hEireann. Few outside the republican community would know Walsh. I knew this wasn't a prank and I told my editors to run with what they had.

"It sounds right to me," I told Colman.

I had previously discussed with him the possibility of the IRA providing some audio or video of its statement.

Within minutes, some order had been restored to the situation. My contact with the IRA leadership appeared in the street earlier than expected and directed Mallie and I towards the back entrance of a house. He followed a few steps behind. Inside, we were each given an envelope containing the two-page IRA statement and the Walsh recording. Mallie left first and I paused for a few moments as "P O'Neill" struggled with the television remote in an effort to show me the DVD. There was nothing I could do to help. I am one of those who has been left behind in the video age. So, I took the statement and the DVD and moved to leave by the front door but was directed out the back. There was no time to talk to the senior IRA leader, to get his thoughts on this big moment in republican history, to get anything other than the two pages of text I had in my hand.

He would have known the mood, and he would have been a key voice in the IRA discussion which had taken the organisation to this point, as he had been a key voice in the republican debate at the time of the Good Friday Agreement. On the rainy streets of west Belfast, I dialled the *Talkback* studio at *Radio Ulster,* and, within a few minutes, I was speaking live to the presenter Wendy Austin. She told me the text the office had was not signed by "P O'Neill", the *nom-de-plume* used by the IRA, but I was able to assure her that he had put his name to the statement I had just been given. It was at the bottom of page two below 59 lines of type, which summarised the IRA debate and told us the outcome of those discussions.

In this statement, the IRA spoke as plainly as Adams did in his April speech. It ordered an end to its armed campaign, ordered its units to dump their arms and instructed its volunteers to assist "in the development of purely political and democratic programmes through exclusively peaceful means". Members of the IRA were told they "must not engage in any other activities whatsoever". The IRA leadership authorised its representative to engage with the   Independent   International   Commission   on Decommissioning to complete the process of putting "arms beyond use", and two churchmen – one a Protestant, the other a Catholic – were invited to witness this process. "P O'Neill" was writing for two audiences.

Yes, it was a statement that would be put under the microscope by the governments and the unionists and every word and every sentence would be checked and double checked for its meaning. But exactly the same would happen inside the IRA. Here, too, every word would be scrutinised by the men and women who had fought the "Brits" over three decades and more.

And, so, the IRA leadership spoke to its own. It reiterated its view that the armed struggle was "entirely legitimate" and restated that it remained "fully committed to the goals of Irish unity and independence and to building the Republic outlined in the 1916 Proclamation".

"It would have been a difficult statement to write, but the

political imperative was that it be written in stark terms."

This is a republican source speaking to me for this book.

"The IRA had to reflect in its words what Gerry Adams had said previously about a peaceful way to a united Ireland," the source continued.

He meant that there could be no conflict between the IRA statement of July and the Adams speech of April, and he accepted that for the British/unionist audience it had to be a statement "without doubt".

"It was really for that audience that this development came about. There was no demand for it within the IRA or the wider republican community. They were content that the IRA was on ceasefire and were dealing with their guns as they saw fit."

He said the leadership was asking the IRA membership to take a "quantum leap" to lift the process out of the "quagmire created by the doubt over previous (IRA) statements". "For the IRA audience it had to be clear as well – (clear) that it (the war) was over," the source said.

"There hadn't to be any trailing doubt as to where the IRA was in its head on the 28th (of July 2005)."

That day as I stood in the rain on the street in west Belfast chatting to Wendy Austin on the *Talkback* show, I watched other journalists, including Ken Reid of *Ulster Television* and Dan McGinn of the *Press Association*, being taken to the house that I had left just minutes earlier. The IRA text, its DVD, these latest words from the Army Council – words of peace, not war – were being moved along a kind of conveyor belt, moved in the direction of the major news outlets and from there into the homes of the listening and watching and reading public.

It may not have emerged the way the IRA had intended, but its statement was now travelling through all the news stations in Ireland, Britain and internationally. The dance was back in step. It was a day I remember in its finest detail.

Kathleen Carragher, the BBC's editor of radio in Belfast, came on the line. It was a couple of minutes to one and she asked me could I do something for the news bulletin. With the rain spitting on my notebook, I quickly jotted down a few thoughts, and, within seconds, Keith Burnside was introducing me on air. From my scribbled note, I said the following:

"This is the script we expected from the IRA. It has ordered the end of the armed campaign. This is as close as you get to the language of the war is over. The decommissioning process is to be completed quickly. Church witnesses are being introduced to give that process more credibility. And, in a sentence, this is the republican reins being handed over from the IRA to Sinn Féin in a move from armed to political struggle."

Then it was back to the office. The television editor Angelina Fusco took the Walsh DVD to get it transferred onto tape and ready for broadcast on the *News 24* channel and, locally, on her *BBC Newsline* programme. And, soon, Séanna Walsh would be speaking out of television sets into the homes of the many who were watching. On this day, a very private republican took on a very public role. Séanna Walsh is a man in his forties who, over two stretches, spent 21 years in prison, in the cages and blocks of the Maze jail – or Long Kesh as republicans call it. He was one of the first republicans to refuse to wear prison clothes and to join what became known as the "blanket protest". When he spoke to me for a radio documentary in 2001, he chose words from Bobby Sands to describe that battle within the jail during the "very darkest days" of the mid-seventies through to the early eighties:

"He described it as the breaker's yard. That's what the administration sought to do with it, to turn it into a breaker's yard for republicanism, that anybody who went through there; that they would break them and send them out as broken men, but we actually managed to turn it against them."

The Belfast republican was in the jail throughout the hunger strike of 1981 when Sands died after refusing food for 66 days. Walsh remembers all of that, and in the radio documentary that I mentioned earlier, he spoke to me about his last letter from Sands, and of the emotional roller-coaster the prisoners were on in those last days of the hunger striker's life:

"I actually had the letter for about three or four years... I kept it for a couple of months, then I sent it out of the jail and it was sitting in a house along with other IRA documents, and the house was raided, and the woman just threw all the IRA documents on the fire and burnt them. So, I lost the last letter that Bobby wrote (to) me."

In the letter, Sands was saying goodbye to Walsh. With the hunger strike there was the inevitability of death, and, in his interview with me, Walsh remembered that moment and Sands' last words to him:

"This is the end of me. Obviously, I'm not telling my family that... But I'm not going to try to pull the wool over your eyes. So, this is goodbye."

Walsh told me if there was any doubt in his mind about where the hunger strike would lead, that last letter from Sands "banished it entirely", but then there was some hope:

"Once he got elected (as an MP in the 1981 by-election in Fermanagh South Tyrone) we didn't believe that he was going to die. We didn't believe that Thatcher would have let him die. Before the hunger strike started, once the hunger strike started, I had absolutely no doubt that Bobby was going to die and neither had he. Once he was elected that changed things but only for a while and, whenever he died, it was a massive blow."

Many years later, Walsh was one of the first IRA prisoners freed early as part of the Good Friday Agreement, and his role since then has been in the background as part of that small trusted "core group" – the negotiating team that works so closely with Adams and McGuinness. There was a brief glimpse of him on the public stage during the summer of 2004 when he emerged from the audience during a debate at the West Belfast Festival to challenge the Democratic Unionist MP Jeffrey Donaldson on the issue of decommissioning. The real question, Walsh asserted, was how you removed the IRA's "capacity" (for war).

"How are you going to remove that capacity, Jeffrey? Are you going to kill me? Because that's the only way you can do it. Unless you reach some sort of agreement with me and people like me, that's the only way that people like me can be defused."

"I had never encountered this man before and didn't know much about him when he asked his question." This is Jeffrey Donaldson speaking to me for this book. "It was only afterwards when I was told who he was that I recognised the significance both of the question and of the person who had posed it. Walsh's significance was further emphasised to me when he appeared to read the IRA statement at the end of July (2005)."

Walsh was making a point that had been made previously by a string of chief constables in Northern Ireland – Sir Hugh Annesley, Sir Ronnie Flanagan and Sir Hugh Orde – that you cannot decommission the engineering knowledge of the IRA. That organisation has always had within its ranks men and women capable of manufacturing a range of improvised weaponry including bombs, mortars, rockets and grenades. There has always been that know-how, the wherewithal to sustain the organisation and to keep it battle-fit and ready.

"Of course it is true that the IRA could decommission all their weapons and still have the capacity through improvisation to produce extremely potent weapons including explosives," Donaldson accepts. "But the point of decommissioning is that it provides tangible evidence of the IRA's true intent."

For unionists, decommissioning was a kind of political comfort blanket, a rather frayed and well-chewed comfort blanket. They knew, as Jeffrey Donaldson had said, that if it wanted to, the IRA could rearm itself and resume its war. But, to help build confidence, unionists needed the republican organisation to destroy the guns and the explosives it had in its bunkers. It would do that in September 2005.

The real challenge for the peace process and for the republican leadership was to do something more than that – something much more significant. It was to decommission the "volunteers" of the IRA, to end their "active service", to offer them a viable and credible alternative to armed struggle, and to achieve this without splitting the organisation. That is what the Adams speech of April was about. This was the republican leadership presenting that argument and that alternative from inside the movement. It was Adams saying to the IRA that there was another way, and the fact that the IRA leadership had pre-knowledge of his speech and let it happen meant the Army Council was with Adams and McGuinness.

This was the only way the argument could be won. It had to be from inside the Republican movement, not from outside it. In the way it was done there could be no suggestion of humiliation or surrender. This was a republican initiative. This was Adams asking the IRA to do something, not the unionists or the British or anyone else telling it to do something. And the response of that organisation would make more possible the type of agreement Walsh had talked about in that moment when he challenged Jeffrey Donaldson.

Yes, the IRA wrote into its statement that the decommissioning process would be completed quickly, and that two churchmen along with the commissioners of the decommissioning body would witness the arms being put beyond use. It had to be said for the unionists. But even if there was such a thing as total decommissioning – and I don't believe there is – it would not remove the IRA's capacity. The political alternative presented by Adams has to flower and the DUP has to do business with republicans. That is the way you remove the IRA's will to fight. And that is what Walsh was talking about when he emerged from the audience in west Belfast, and, when, as an IRA man he spoke directly to a senior member of Ian Paisley's party. In how things are developing here, it was another significant moment – and something that would not have been possible just a few years ago.

In an interview for this book on October 3, 2005 – just a week after General de Chastelain reported that the IRA had now completed the process of putting its arms beyond use – I spoke to the chief constable Sir Hugh Orde on this issue of decommissioning versus capacity.

ORDE: It's mindsets versus mortars. For me what was important, what is important, is that the guns don't get used... The availability of guns is probably wider than it has ever been before, and if you've got good systems you can get guns. Never mind, you don't need guns, you can get blown up here without any guns. They've got the technology. So, the issue is around going back to war or not. So, I think from a policing perspective, I wasn't that fussed about it. I think it was vital, because it was around reassurance and underpinning the commitment they'd (the IRA) given some time before. But I wasn't going to get terribly excited about decommissioning and, I think the way it played, decommissioning wasn't seen as some huge step forward... It was around wait and see, and I'm waiting to see what they do next.

ROWAN: But their capacity is not damaged, is that what you are saying?

ORDE: Well, I don't think you damage capacity by removing (weapons) from an organisation like that... You may damage it short term, but I think short term is pretty short term. It's also based on the assumption that everything (meaning all weapons) is gone... I was slightly surprised by de Chastelain saying all their arms... Do the IRA know what the totality of their arms are?... If you take it at face value, it's a positive event.

ROWAN: Confidence building.

ORDE: Providing the politicians on the other side allow it to build confidence, then it is a step in the right direction, but no more in my judgement. What it has done, of course, is put pressure on other organisations to disarm now.

On Thursday, July 28, as the IRA statement and the Walsh DVD began to emerge publicly, I got a message on my mobile phone from Tony Blair's Downing Street spokesman Tom Kelly, my one-time colleague at the BBC. It arrived at fourteen minutes past one, and the text read:

"Cow now in space."

I knew exactly what he meant. In the way that I had described the '94 ceasefire as the political equivalent of the cow actually jumping over the moon, eleven years on, Kelly was using that same thought to describe the significance of this latest IRA statement. Downing Street and Blair and his chief of staff, Jonathan Powell, had finally got the IRA statement they had been waiting for, and Kelly's message was making that clear. Soon, Blair would speak for himself. He welcomed the clarity of the IRA statement and described it as "a step of unparalleled magnitude in the recent history of Northern Ireland". Blair accepted that the statement ended the IRA's campaign and so too did the Irish Taoiseach Bertie Ahern. He said he hoped and believed that this would mark the day when the tradition of violence finally came to an end.

"This statement is unprecedented," Ahern said. "If the IRA's words are borne out by verified actions, it will be a momentous and historic development."

Republicans also understood the meaning and significance of the statement. Within hours of its release, the last IRA jail leader freed from the Maze – the Belfast republican Jim McVeigh – put it in this context:

"The war's over," he said. "The IRA have said the war's over, but the struggle isn't over. We still believe as strongly in the (republican) objectives as we did a year ago, or five years ago or ten years ago, and it's about intensifying the struggle by bringing more people into the struggle as far as we're concerned."

Jim McVeigh was speaking to my colleague Tara Mills on the *BBC Newsline* programme at teatime on Thursday July 28. Just a couple of hours earlier, I had bumped into him on the Falls Road and asked him would he do the interview. Sitting beside him was Rosie McCorley, a former leader of IRA women prisoners in another of the jails – Maghaberry. Of all of the republican initiatives, she said, this was the biggest one to date.

"This initiative is historic from the IRA. Obviously we want to find a peaceful resolution to this conflict, and to do that we need to bring that about with the unionist community. So, the unionist community, I think, have nothing to fear from this statement and, if they read it carefully, they'll see the genuine commitment that there is from the IRA and from republicans. But there is a big obligation and duty on the leadership of the unionist community, in terms of the DUP, which is the biggest party now, and they've got to fulfil their obligations towards their community in terms of bringing about a resolution to this conflict," she said.

The DUP leader Ian Paisley is not rushing to make any judgements about this statement. He still wonders what the IRA is up to, still doesn't believe it, still needs to be convinced that this is for real, and will take time to be persuaded. For him decommissioning is only one part of the test he has set for the IRA. He wants its structure collapsed and all activities to end, and he is asking himself what the IRA is going to do with those who have been a part of that organisation.

"What worried me was not so much the decommissioning. What worried me was what was coming after," Ian Paisley told me. "What are they going to offer their volunteers? They must offer them something. They can't say we saw you in prison; we carried your coffins to the graveyard, because you died on hunger strike and all of that. I mean there's bound to be feeling in the IRA, there's bound to be feeling that we better watch we'll not be sold, and I don't know how they would get over that."

So Paisley has still to be convinced that the IRA is going to go away and can go away. But this was, as Rosie McCorley described it, the biggest IRA initiative of the peace process, bigger than the ceasefires and bigger than the three acts of decommissioning that had taken place up to this point. What this statement was doing was paving the way for what I think is an inevitable political agreement between Sinn Féin and the Democratic Unionist Party, however long that might take. It was also taking republicans ever closer to endorsing the new policing arrangements in Northern Ireland. This is the reading between the lines of the IRA statement. It wasn't just about signalling the end of its war. This was the IRA and the wider Republican movement strategically placing themselves for the next phase of the peace process.

To get to that phase, only months after the biggest bank robbery in UK history and just weeks after the British capital was visited by suicide bombers, the IRA had to speak and act in an unprecedented way. It was unprecedented in the current republican campaign both in terms of the clarity of the text released by P O'Neill and also in relation to the scale of the planned decommissioning, which we were told would be completed and be seen by additional witnesses. But, whatever the immediate context, in terms of the events that preceded the July 28 statement, a republican initiative on this scale was quietly being considered since the early summer of the previous year and probably for longer. This is something I will return to later.

The decision of the IRA was not a unanimous one. The intelligence assessment of the debate suggested the "hearts and minds" of the organisation took some time to explain to people "this is the way it is, this is the way we're going, this is the reason for it". But, according to this assessment, "not everybody accepted".

ROWAN: Not everybody?

SENIOR INTELLIGENCE OFFICER: No. There are places in the province (where) historically the Belfast writ doesn't run. There are parts of mid Ulster and Tyrone which are at the heartland of what I call traditional rural republicanism that don't … have the viewpoint of the "sophisticates"…

ROWAN: They had to be told?

SENIOR INTELLIGENCE OFFICER: I think some places were told this is the way it's going, and there's been a variety of responses from across the province.

The IRA organisation will take time to absorb the significance of the July statement. On paper it is the ending of the "Long War" – a stepping back from armed struggle and a move away from the gun. In this latest phase of the peace process, Adams and McGuinness have again succeeded in persuading the IRA to take further significant steps – its most significant steps so far in terms of the words it chose to speak and its acts of decommissioning. Those moves were a further endorsement of the Adams and McGuinness leadership. But, now, before the politics can move on, there has to be the proving of what has been said and done – this pause, if you like in some "testing period" of unknown duration. What the IRA has done is something that can only be assessed over time. But, what can be said already is that it has done significantly more than the loyalist organisations both in terms of decommissioning and ending its violent activities.

In the days and weeks after the IRA's July statement, the peace process witnessed a kind of political and paramilitary earthquake inside the Protestant community. Before decommissioning, the IRA's words had to be matched by British military action. The Army announced a two-year plan to end "Operation Banner", its decades-long support role to the police in Northern Ireland. With this the home-based battalions of the Royal Irish Regiment – which grew out of the Ulster Defence Regiment (UDR) – would be stood down. Almost immediately, work began on dismantling army watchtowers in south Armagh, west Belfast and Derry. It had the appearance of "military Brits out".

"At no stage did they consult us about what they were doing," said DUP deputy leader Peter Robinson, speaking to me for this book. "The handling of the concessions that they gave to the IRA was appalling as well... The Royal Irish, I mean some Ulster Unionists were saying, 'Well, how long did the DUP know?' Ian Paisley got a phone call from (the Defence Secretary) John Reid five minutes after you people in the BBC had already announced it on the news. That's how much notice we were given of that."

Days later, three republicans on the run from the Colombian authorities surfaced in Ireland and, weeks after that, there was an explosion of loyalist violence linked to a disputed Orange march in west Belfast. Secretary of State Peter Hain was forced to end the political farce of continuing to recognise the ceasefires of the UVF and the linked Red Hand Commando. One veteran loyalist described what was happening as the outworking of an anti-Good Friday Agreement diatribe that had been instilled into the Protestant community. At ground level, he said, this had created a perception that "the Taigs (Catholics) were getting everything, and the Prods (Protestants), nothing".

"Those who are supposed to be the pillars of our society are playing on that – using it," my source said. "You have to question the leadership of unionism, and I include the Orange Order in that."

The peace process was about to ask the biggest questions yet of the unionist/loyalist leaderships, and we were about to see if that initial reaction to the IRA statement, and what developed from it, was the storm before the calm. I will deal with all of this in greater detail later. But why should we be so confident that an eventual deal between Paisley and the "Provos" now seems inevitable? I suppose, because against all expectations they came so close to doing it in 2004, and because the way people are now voting in Northern Ireland means that for both parties, the only route to power and to government is in doing political business with each other.

CHAPTER TWO

TALKING EYES, SILENT PHOTOGRAPHS

"The IRA needs to be humiliated and they need to wear their sackcloth and ashes not in a back room but openly, and we have no apology for the stand we are taking." DUP leader Ian Paisley, November 27, 2004, stressing the need for photographic proof of decommissioning.

"For his part, Ian Paisley demanded that our contribution be photographed and reduced to an act of humiliation. This was never possible...We restate our commitment to the peace process. But we will not submit to a process of humiliation." P O'Neill, December 9, 2004.

"It was pretty clear to us that they failed the sincerity test, and put it like this, a few tough words from the 'Big Man' of unionism wasn't really going to hurt the great Oglaigh na hEireann." Ian Paisley junior, October 2005, defending his father's "sackcloth and ashes" speech.

"The two governments were told that I had broached the issue of the photographs and the IRA had said no. So, for them then to have gone on and given Ian Paisley the prospect that there would be photographs was folly of the worst kind." Sinn Féin's chief negotiator Martin McGuinness, speaking in October 2005.

It was the most ambitious political project of the peace process – even bigger than the Good Friday Agreement. This time the players were different. The players were Paisley and the Provos. John Hume with his senior colleagues in the SDLP – Seamus Mallon and Mark Durkan – brought political power-sharing back in the 1998 negotiation with David Trimble, a huge achievement in itself. Trimble is gone now from the main political stage, on which Sir Reg Empey is the new Ulster Unionist Party leader. But in terms of votes and seats and significance, Paisley is the leader of unionism in the political arena beyond the Good Friday Agreement. If he wants to be First Minister, if he wants to bow out of politics in that high position, then he will have to make a deal with Adams and McGuinness. It is his only route to power and to government in Northern Ireland. Over many months, in many long hours of discussions, they tried for this in 2004. It was a period of talking and not talking – a phase in this process that would produce stories of bugging, of a broken-down deal and then a bank job. And for weeks and weeks, we talked about photographs that would never be taken – and therefore could never be seen.

At first, they seemed to be working on the impossible – on what was once the unthinkable. It was a negotiation at arms length. Sinn Féin was talking to the British and Irish governments and so too was the DUP. Months earlier, the political dynamics in Northern Ireland had changed – changed after another failed negotiation involving Adams and the then Ulster Unionist leader David Trimble in late 2003, and changed after an election to a suspended political institution just a few weeks later. That election to the Northern Ireland Assembly in November 2003 catapulted the Democratic Unionist Party and Sinn Féin into the lead political roles in their respective communities – positions they have since consolidated and built upon. So, the business of deal-making is now primarily a matter for them.

The first public utterances were not encouraging. The DUP

leader told us the Good Friday Agreement was finished, and Adams said he believed that Paisley would try to wreck that historic deal. He warned the British Government not to allow the process to develop on Paisley's terms. These were the initial verbal punches they exchanged in public but, behind the scenes, and at a distance from each other, Sinn Féin and the DUP were exploring with the governments a possible way forward. Significant progress was being made and, if it worked, it would be the deal of all deals because of who was involved.

Adams needed to tread carefully. The failure of the negotiations in 2003 was still fresh in the mind of the IRA. The republican organisation believed that Trimble and the two governments had reneged on an agreement – an agreement in which the IRA had spoken and acted in the belief that the power-sharing Executive at Stormont would be restored. It was suspended in October 2002 after the IRA was linked to a robbery at Special Branch offices in Belfast and to intelligence-gathering activities inside the Northern Ireland Office. So, the purpose of the 2003 negotiations was to rebuild the political process and to try to get words and actions from the IRA that would finally convince Trimble and the unionist community that the republican organisation was leaving the stage.

If a deal could be done, it would be built around a joint declaration by the two governments which would deal not just with the politics but with other issues including policing, demilitarisation and inquiries into controversial killings, including the murders of the solicitors Pat Finucane and Rosemary Nelson – a key demand of both Sinn Féin and the SDLP.

In the period from April through to October 2003, there were several IRA statements and a number of speeches by Adams, but the language here was nothing like as clear as the words later spoken by "P O'Neill" in July 2005. In a statement passed to the two governments on April 13 2003, the IRA said it was "resolved to see the complete and final closure" of the conflict. It also said it was "determined to ensure that our activities, disciplines and strategies will be consistent with this".

"Furthermore, the full and irreversible implementation of the Agreement (Good Friday Agreement) and other commitments (in the Joint Declaration) will provide a context in which the IRA can proceed to definitively set aside arms to further our political objectives. When there is such a context this decision can be taken only by a General Army Convention representing all IRA volunteers."

In July 2005, the IRA formally ordered an end to its armed campaign without such a Convention.

The April '03 statement prompted the two governments to look for meanings inside the republican dictionary. There was both a public and a private process of clarification, as Blair and Ahern played "What Does That Mean?" with Adams and McGuinness. Twice in April, at Stormont and on the Falls Road, Adams gave public clarification. He said the IRA statement was "a statement of completely peaceful intent", and that in the decommissioning process the IRA intended to put all, and not just some, of its arms beyond use. This was the Sinn Féin President speaking on April 27. Three days later he spoke again.

"The IRA leadership is determined that there will be no activities which will undermine in any way the peace process and the Good Friday Agreement."

On May 6, the IRA said Adams had accurately reflected its position, but there was no deal now and there would be no deal at the second attempt in October.

This time, however, Adams and the IRA believed they were part of an agreed sequence of statements and events which also involved Trimble, the two governments and the Independent International Commission on Decommissioning (IICD). The day of this sequence was October 21 2003 – a day that would mark the beginning of the end of Trimble as the major unionist player in the peace process. The man who had been such a key figure in the negotiations leading to the Good Friday Agreement and who had shared the Nobel Peace Prize with John Hume would soon be brushed aside by the unionist electorate. The DUP's moment was arriving, and so too was the day that would require a Paisley-Provo deal if the politics of this place were to work again.

The IRA's understanding of the October 21 sequence was this:

- The announcement of an election (to the Northern Ireland Assembly on November 26);
- a statement by Gerry Adams;
- a statement from the IRA leadership;
- an act of putting arms beyond use (involving the largest amount of arms to date);
- a report by the IICD;
- a statement by David Trimble;
- a joint statement by the two governments.

Five of the seven steps had been taken when Trimble emerged at his party's headquarters in east Belfast to put the sequence "on hold". The Ulster Unionist leader had not heard enough about the scale of the IRA's third act of decommissioning and was not prepared to proceed with a statement outlining his party's desire to see the power-sharing Executive restored. The sequence had stalled and an election had already been publicly announced.

Earlier that day, Adams had done most of the republican talking. He said he was totally committed to playing a leadership role to bring an end to conflict including physical force republicanism.

"Our strategy to do this is based on creating a purely peaceful and alternative way to achieve democratic and republican objectives," the Sinn Féin President said. And then he repeated what P O'Neill had said back in that April statement.

"The IRA leadership wants the full and irreversible implementation of the Good Friday Agreement in all its aspects and they are determined that their strategies and actions will be consistent with this objective. Implementation by the two governments and the parties of their commitments under the Agreement provides the context in which Irish republicans and unionists will, as equals, pursue their objectives peacefully, thus providing full and final closure of the conflict... As President of Sinn Féin, I have set out a peaceful direction which I trust everyone will follow."

The IRA welcomed the Adams speech and again said that he had accurately reflected its position. That should not surprise us. Given the leadership position he holds, Adams would always know the mind of the IRA Army Council, particularly on matters relating to the peace process. In its October 21 statement, that leadership said its third act of decommissioning would be verified by the IICD "under the agreed scheme" – a scheme which prohibited General John de Chastelain and his Commission colleague Andrew Sens from speaking publicly in any detail about the process. The republican words of October were more or less the same as those that had been spoken just a few months earlier, the decommissioning process was unchanged and so too was the outcome of this latest negotiation.

Trimble had not been brought to the point of publicly endorsing a return to government, and the backdrop to an election – now just weeks away – was another broken down deal. The DUP would thrive in that election and Trimble's party would lose its lead role in the unionist community. These were the changing dynamics which created the circumstances in which Paisley and the "Provos" would be asked to try to do business with each other – to bring back the power-sharing Executive that was born in that negotiation of 1998.

In the November 2003 election the DUP won 30 seats and the Ulster Unionists 27, but the real damage was done when the MP Jeffrey Donaldson and two of his UUP colleagues defected to the DUP. Paisley's party now had 33 seats, Trimble's just 24, and this trend would continue through future elections. It was the same on the nationalist side. Sinn Féin now had 24 seats, the SDLP 18. The major parties at the time of the Good Friday Agreement were now being squeezed and Adams and Paisley had been elevated to significantly stronger positions. As the negotiations developed in the months after November 2003, we began to see the roots of the IRA's July 2005 initiative. Something on the grand scale and clarity of that moment was being contemplated for months and months, long before the Northern Bank robbery and the Robert McCartney murder. But it was a negotiation in which the DUP made one demand too many and Paisley made one speech too many. In words he spoke in November 2004, and in his party's demand for visual proof of decommissioning, the chance of that once unthinkable political deal was lost. That said the circumstances that would be needed to pull together these now dominant political forces would be re-created later in this process.

The political talking after the November '03 election stretched out over the best part of a year. Blair's Chief of Staff, Jonathan Powell, along with the political director at the Northern Ireland Office Jonathan Phillips and his deputy Robert Hannigan were the senior British officials involved. In a conversation with me, a DUP source described Powell as the "strategist, (the) wheeler-dealer" in the negotiations. Phillips, he said, was more about "detail" and the "nuances of Northern Ireland politics", and, in these talks, he said, he trusted Phillips' judgement. A republican view of Phillips was that he was one of those who believed that the process could only go as fast as unionism would let it go.

"That is a very firm view of ours," a source told me.

Michael Collins from the Taoiseach's office headed the Irish team – which included Brendan Scannell, Adrian O'Neill, and Tim Dalton – and, separately, Sinn Féin and the DUP were talking to both governments in a negotiation that would often reach up to prime ministerial level and involve Blair and Ahern. For them this peace process has been an eight-year project of political ups and downs. The DUP wanted to change the Good Friday Agreement to make the ministers more accountable in the power-sharing Executive – more accountable to their cabinet colleagues. They also wanted the First and Deputy First Ministers appointed through a different voting mechanism and, at the top of government, they wanted less "jointery" so to speak.

In other words the DUP was not ready to put up its hand to vote for Sinn Féin and not yet ready for Ian Paisley and Martin McGuinness to be paraded in the shape of conjoined political twins in the roles of First and Deputy First Ministers.

"The DUP do not have confidence in Sinn Féin ministers, therefore why should they be asked to put up their hand for a Sinn Féin minister," said Peter Robinson to me in an interview for this book.

"We're not the ones that are insisting on having a mandatory coalition; therefore we shouldn't be asked to approve of ministers that we do not have confidence in."

So, a way had to be found to soften this blow for a party which had once boasted it would "smash" Sinn Féin. The huge issue of policing, and how to win republican support for the police service and the board tasked with ensuring accountability, was another matter to be settled.

Sinn Féin wanted policing and justice powers transferred to local politicians in a new ministry at Stormont. And, for the DUP, this brought with it the nightmare of Gerry Kelly – a convicted IRA bomber and jail escaper – having some future political role in law and order.

To open the door to these new possibilities, republicans had to find a way to remove the IRA from the equation and, in the early summer of 2004, I began to hear the first hints of this type of thinking. Republicans knew the dangers in this. Paisley, in his way of doing things, would undoubtedly revel in any circumstances which would allow him to claim that he had brought the IRA to the table of democracy, or more likely in his words, to the table of surrender. And, how he would relish a political moment in which he could say, not quietly but loudly, that he had succeeded where Trimble had failed. Yes, the DUP might have to swallow hard to do business with Sinn Féin, but much of what was being considered would stick in the republican throat. Doing a deal with the "No" man of Ulster politics would require the IRA to say and do much more than it said and did for Trimble. But then Paisley, unlike Trimble, was more capable of making a deal that would stick, not just in his craw, but in a way that would deliver working politics. The DUP was not interested in political hot housing – or in high wire summits – and was adamant that it would not be bounced into an agreement, something it would accuse the governments of attempting to do later in this negotiation.

"The DUP were most anxious to give the impression to the two governments and, through the two governments, most anxious to give us the impression that they were up for a deal," said Sinn Féin's chief negotiator Martin McGuinness.

McGUINNESS: So, as always we explore these situations. We deal with them very seriously indeed, and obviously recognised that to bring about a circumstance whereby Ian Paisley would be in a power-sharing administration, and just as importantly in the All Ireland Ministerial Council alongside the Taoiseach, other ministers from Dublin and ourselves, was the story of the century if we could bring that about. So, we were very determined to play our part in making that happen, that against the backdrop of all sorts of sniping from the SDLP on the sidelines. But, to be quite honest, the SDLP only saw the wee picture. We were looking at the big picture.

One of the SDLP's senior negotiators, the party's policing spokesman, Alex Attwood, dismisses that as nonsense.

"Martin McGuinness makes that claim because that's the only

way he can explain away the fact that... Sinn Féin were negotiating with the DUP a worse deal for nationalists than the SDLP negotiated with the UUP in 1998. So, if I were Martin McGuinness I would be trying to explain away the weakness of their negotiation by saying they saw the big picture. The second reason why McGuinness is saying what he said is that they made a huge strategic mistake when they went public as Gerry Adams did in the *Irish Times* saying that Sinn Féin were willing to suspend their scepticism about DUP intentions, quote unquote. Now once the DUP saw that, they knew that the Good Friday Agreement was in play and then they began to unpick it. And they got a sign of weakness from Sinn Féin – a sign that the SDLP never sent to the UUP in all our negotiations," said Attwood.

By mid June 2004, there was further confirmation of the new political realities in Northern Ireland. Paisley chose not to contest the European elections. The DUP candidate was Jim Allister who, when the counting was done, had almost twice as many votes as the Ulster Unionist Jim Nicholson. The gap was huge – Allister 175,761 votes, Nicholson 91,164. Sinn Féin's Mary Lou McDonald had already won a seat in Dublin when, across the border, Bairbre de Brun took a second for her party. Her tally of votes was 144,541 with the SDLP's Martin Morgan on 87,559. Those who in the political process had been hoping for an Ulster Unionist/SDLP revival would not have seen it in these results, and it was becoming even more obvious where the business of deal-making would have to be done. It was a week after the election that I heard the first suggestions from a republican of an initiative that could see the IRA leave the stage.

"We want that excuse (of the IRA) removed from the British and the unionists," he told me. "Now what that means in practical terms is for us to work out in these negotiations."

Our conversation was on June 21. He said the positions being worked on had to be "conclusive, definitive" and he believed the DUP would know through the governments that republicans were interested in a deal which would include an end to "physical force republicanism". At this stage, there was no suggestion that there was an IRA text in the negotiations, but my source said that when one emerged it would have to be written in words that did not require spin. What was being considered was the clearest IRA statement on its future and the most significant acts of decommissioning so far. Definitive, conclusive, final, was the language being used to describe the work of this latest negotiation, and those involved needed to agree not just the deal but how it would be verified and what would fill the gap between the IRA making its contribution and the Executive being restored.

The two governments in their discussions with the DUP and Sinn Féin were trying to agree proposals for a comprehensive agreement – what I call the deal of all deals.

Twenty-four hours later, I travelled to the home of a senior DUP politician. It was impossible to report on what the IRA might do if I didn't also know the mind of his party. We met just after four o'clock on June 22 and we chatted in his study. He told me if a deal developed out of these negotiations then the IRA's "bluff" would be called first.

"Before we go into government, decommissioning will be completed," he told me.

He said the DUP had a policy that required "total decommissioning and an end to paramilitarism".

"They (the IRA) would be entering into a deal contingent on these things. Bluffing us doesn't do them any good. If they are saying to us – through government – that they can deliver, their bluff will be called before ours. I don't think they would enter into the deal if it was going to fall apart on these issues."

This would not be a deal like the many others in this process – the deals that were squeezed into a sequence of events over twenty-four to forty-eight hours and that played out in dramatic fashion. This time things would be very different. There would be a gap between what the IRA said and did – a testing period –

before the DUP would enter government with Sinn Féin. This was already understood by the time I had this conversation – although that is not to say that it had been accepted by republicans.

In the testing period, there would be reports by the Independent Monitoring Commission – a kind of ceasefire watchdog. The DUP would read these for proof that the IRA had switched off all activities – that, this time, it had genuinely gone away.

The party would also want to hear the assessment of the Chief Constable and, critical to any deal-making, would be the report of the Independent International Commission on Decommissioning. My source told me that decommissioning was not about convincing de Chastelain, but was about convincing unionists. And he stressed the need for clarity in what the IRA would say about its future, or more accurately I suppose its non-future.

"If we have to reach for the decoding manual, the game is lost. There is a bluntness about the unionists that requires it to be straightforward," he said.

All of this was possible but, in this conversation, my source also repeated the DUP demand for "a visual context" to decommissioning. His party wanted film or photographs of the IRA's decommissioned weapons. This was the one demand too many that was made in this negotiation. At no stage did I hear anything from republicans to suggest it was possible but, right up to the dying moments of these talks in December 2004, some believed it was. In the five-month period from June through to then, I was in regular contact with this senior DUP source and other members of his party.

In June, I also had a conversation with my colleague Gareth Gordon – one of the BBC's political team in Belfast – and I shared with him that comment that republicans were working on removing the "excuse" of the IRA. Weeks later, he would hear this line repeated, not quietly as it had been said to me, but out loud in an interview with the Sinn Féin President Gerry Adams on August 5.

"I personally feel that while there are justifiable fears within unionism about the IRA, I think political unionism uses the IRA and the issue of IRA arms as an excuse," Adams told my colleague. "I think that republicans need to be prepared to remove that as an excuse. But we who are in leadership will only be empowered to do so if there is a context in which we can make progress."

Gordon knew the significance of what Adams was saying, and whether he said it deliberately or whether it was just something that came out in this interview didn't really matter. We knew from that conversation back in June, that removing that "excuse" was what the republican negotiating team was thinking about and working on.

In news reports that evening, I said: "Just weeks ahead of crucial political negotiations, Gerry Adams is saying a number of things. (1): That he is prepared to try to persuade the IRA to make its most significant moves in this process so far. But, (2): That that will only be possible if others do their bit – the most significant others being the governments and the DUP. What's being worked on is 'the deal of all deals'. Within months the governments would want to say that the IRA has gone and there would have to be the most significant acts of decommissioning so far. But what are the other key ingredients? Agreement on demilitarisation and policing; and working politics at Stormont and elsewhere. Nothing is certain, nothing is agreed, but some believe a once unthinkable deal is becoming a possibility."

On August 5, Adams had thought out loud, too loud for many in the IRA. Internally, there was a "substantial kickback". The organisation was not ready, or prepared, for the "implications" of the Adams commentary – the implications being a redundant IRA. One source told me the interview had caused "massive problems for the Council (IRA Army Council)" and that these problems were right across the organisation.

Was this one of Adams' rare slips in this process, that he spoke publicly before the necessary internal preparatory work had been done?

Internally, the IRA had to be settled, work that falls to a small number of trusted and senior IRA figures close to the Adams-McGuinness negotiating team. These men are Belfast republicans – the IRA's adjutant general, its director of intelligence, former jail leaders at key moments in the "struggle" and another senior member of the organisation who has taken on a prominent role in the parading issue. For Adams and McGuinness they are touchstones – men who take the pulse of the IRA and who know the mood. While this settling and explaining and listening was going on, the minds of the negotiating team were clearly focused on an initiative that would unblock the process – that would open the door into its next phase. To open that door, republicans accepted that they would have to find and then use words that "in the most high risk way" would sell whatever the IRA was prepared to do. Inside the Sinn Féin negotiating team, I think it was now accepted that part of the mistake, in terms of the failure of the October '03 deal, was that republicans had not used words to fully explain the significance of what had happened. On what was said publicly, no one outside the IRA and the IICD could tell how much more significant that third act of decommissioning had been compared to the other two. And it seemed that the mistake of that period was a lesson learned given what was now being contemplated.

The negotiations were now moving towards planned talks at Leeds Castle in Kent in mid-September. There would be three days of meetings. Blair and Ahern would be there, their officials, the DUP and Sinn Féin, David Trimble and Mark Durkan and the other usual participants in these political set pieces. The road to this point was through another difficult summer marching season, and two parades – one in west Belfast and the other in the north of the city – had been particularly difficult. In the lead up to the Whiterock Orange march in late June, all sorts of dire predictions were being made about loyalist violence if the parade was not allowed to follow its planned route onto the nationalist Springfield Road. There had been an original ruling from the Parades Commission – the body that decides on these matters – to prevent the march from doing so, but that decision was reversed at the last minute. A year later, there would be an explosion of loyalist violence linked to a ruling on this same parade, and paramilitaries – supposedly on ceasefire – would turn their guns on police officers and soldiers. The other difficult march during the summer of 2004 was at Ardoyne in north Belfast. This was in July. The parade passes Catholic homes on its way to, and on its return from, the main Twelfth demonstration in the city. A massive police and army operation is needed to get it through, and it passes along a kind of metal security corridor of screens and trucks and other vehicles. In the evening, as the parade returned, there was serious rioting in nationalist Ardoyne. The security forces were attacked and, at one point, a small group of soldiers was surrounded by a hostile crowd. I watched it unfold, and I saw senior republicans including Gerry Kelly and Bobby Storey intervene and put themselves between the soldiers and the crowd. Others saw what happened and others knew the danger of the situation.

Martin McGuinness told me: "We saw a situation where people like Gerry Kelly and other republicans in Belfast city, and obviously ably assisted by republicans in Ardoyne, were effectively placed in the front line of trying to keep the peace in a totally impossible situation where emotions were effectively all over the place."

ROWAN: There was a view that they saved soldiers' lives that night.
McGUINNESS: They saved lives. They saved lives of the community in Ardoyne. For all we know, they saved the lives of unionists in that part of Belfast, and British soldiers who

were on the ground, also, I think, had their lives saved by the very courageous leadership that was shown by Gerry Kelly in the face of just raw emotion. And it was obvious to me at that stage that we were seeing the beginning of another Drumcree and the beginning of another situation which would see the unionists and the Orange Order losing, however long it would take, that ultimately this type of conflict and violence could not be allowed to continue, and that the end result of all of that, at some stage, would be that they would lose Ardoyne in the same way that they lost Drumcree. So, all of that played very badly from our point of view in terms of what we were trying to do, because, right throughout the whole of that period, there were consistent messages coming from the two governments that they believed that Paisley wanted to do a deal. Now, obviously, in trying to make assessments on all of that, you have to factor into it, well if Paisley wants to do a deal, what's Paisley doing to try to minimise conflict in Ardoyne and in north Belfast and in other parts of the North? And, from my point of view, it was obvious to me that there was a conflict between what we were being told and what was happening on the ground... that there was a stark contrast between what was happening in Ardoyne, the way Orangeism was playing itself into that, the way Paisley was standing back from it, the way the governments were, as they are inclined to do in those situations, give into all sorts of loyalist threats and the threats of loyalist paramilitaries. So, obviously we breathed a huge sigh of relief when the Orange marching season was over, and that effectively led us up to Leeds Castle.

It is on this marching issue that loyalists still believe that republicans are at war with them – an "unarmed" war.

Senior loyalist leader Jackie McDonald said: "I have been asked if the IRA really wanted peace, and I do think that they want to control the peace. Any of these contentious parades, Sinn Féin say: No they are not walking down there. The Parades Commission agrees with them and Hugh Orde comes along and says: 'Well I'll implement that'."

There have been decisions by the Parades Commission and by the Chief Constable that republicans have hated. But that is ignored in these comments by McDonald. What he sees is some grand conspiracy being worked against the loyalist community:

"So all that leaves Orangemen and loyalists is frustration; you know, there's this conspiracy against them to try to get them infighting amongst themselves again, to cause problems in their own areas. It turns the loyalist people against the loyalist paramilitaries, and that means in the eventuality, if they ever did think of (another 1974 Ulster Workers) strike situation or massive protest, that loyalism wouldn't all come together, because they've divided them."

So, Whiterock and Ardoyne showed themselves again to be difficult dates on the marching calendar. The summer of 2004 had not passed quietly, but on the scale of what had happened in previous years, it was not as bad as it could have been, and no one was saying that the IRA had orchestrated the violence in north Belfast. Indeed, some were applauding republicans – including Gerry Kelly and Bobby Storey – for their actions in saving the soldiers in that riot situation in north Belfast.

"There were some ugly moments and things were tense," a British Military spokesman said. "While those people showing restraint may not wish to be acknowledged by us, I am bound to say: 'Fair play for intervening'."

Over many years Kelly and Storey as IRA men had been at war with the "Brits". Now they were being applauded and their life-saving actions acknowledged. It is one more example of the peace that was slowly developing.

As the Leeds Castle talks approached, there were obvious signs of irritation and impatience around the negotiations. At one point, Adams accused the DUP of trying to set the bar – in terms of its demands – at heaven's height. The DUP wanted to know what the IRA was prepared to contribute, and it wanted to see the republican text.

"We are past hints," one source told me. "We want to see it. Clarity is important."

There had been a couple of bad-tempered news conferences featuring party leader Ian Paisley in full flow, and, behind the scenes, I was being told that "the Doc" was becoming increasingly impatient. The DUP had been "waiting and waiting and waiting" for sight of an IRA statement.

"As time goes on, Doc has come to the view that it is never going to come, and he becomes more and more sceptical about whether it will ever come in the definitive terms that would be required," a senior party source told me at the time.

The IRA and Adams were not going to rush into business with Paisley. For them, this was not a one-item negotiation. If it was to be a comprehensive agreement, then there were political, policing, military and other matters to be sorted as well. This was the mood as the Leeds Castle talks neared, and then there was a moment of political drama and theatre. It was September 14, and the republican I was speaking to told me it was probably "the biggest bug" he had ever seen. This was not your usual creepy-crawly. It was a mixture of wires, batteries and other gadgetry. This was the stuff of the intelligence war. The ears of the "Brits" and the "Branch" were still listening in to conversations at Connolly House – a Sinn Féin office at Andersonstown in west Belfast. There had been a republican "bug hunt" after a device was found just eight days earlier at the home of a member of Gerry Adams' staff. Now, there was this. Adams was told about the latest find just after meeting with senior British and Irish officials – part of the preparatory talks for the now imminent Leeds Castle negotiations. The bug was then put on show at a news conference inside Connolly House, where the Sinn Féin President accused the British Government of a serious act of bad faith.

"It highlights the continuing hypocrisy of a British system which uses its enormous resources to spy on its political opponents," Adams said. "It is also evidence of the 'war mentality' among the securocrats who run the Northern Ireland Office and whose only engagement with the peace process is to subvert and undermine it. The question is who authorised this and how many more exist?"

The bug was taken to Leeds Castle and the British were asked to explain. It was shown to the Prime Minister and the Taoiseach who were with their officials. I'm told that at first, there was some confusion over something long and thin that was with the bug. Could it be an aerial of some description? The answer was No. It turned out to be a fishing rod – a present from Sinn Féin for the retiring Irish official Tim Dalton. In describing that bug moment in the castle, one source told me: "There was a bit of theatre about it. Everybody knew the game that was being played."

The bug had been in the Connolly House building for years. Indeed, it had listened in on a meeting of the Sinn Féin negotiating team back in July 2001. This was during a break in talks at Weston Park – the type of talks that were now about to be repeated at Leeds Castle. Senior Special Branch and other police officers knew the meeting was being listened to. This specific eavesdropping operation lasted several hours. Late into the night, it was still being transcribed and, before the talks resumed at Weston Park on July 13, a report was sent to MI5. In the midst of the negotiations back then, the British Government knew the mind of the Sinn Féin leadership.

Three years later the bug was found. The Sinn Féin negotiating team had long since stopped using Connolly House for its meetings but, as Leeds Castle approached and with the IRA certain to be the focus of attention, republicans now had something to hit the "Brits" over the head with – not one bug, but two. Adams, of course, would know the realities of the intelligence war. Long after its ceasefire, the IRA was still at it –

inside the Special Branch office at Castlereagh and inside the Northern Ireland Office.

It is a battle in which the pendulum swings, one way and then the other. So, at different times, different sides will have an advantage. This was Adams' turn but, in truth, republicans would have been much more surprised – shocked even – if the British were not listening to them. Bugs and other intelligence-gathering methods were all still part and parcel of a conflict not yet fully settled. It was, as I described it earlier, a moment of political theatre, but these finds were not going to damage the prospects for a deal. The big obstacle that still stood in the way of that was the continuing DUP demand for photographic proof of decommissioning – not just one picture, but a full sequence of snaps.

By mid-September, and with the Leeds Castle talks scheduled to run from the 16th through to the 18th, there was no real sense that this negotiation was yet ready to produce a result in terms of the hoped-for comprehensive agreement. Indeed on the eve of those discussions, a republican source described the various position papers as "vague". The negotiation had not yet moved away from "nod and wink and might and possibly", and the jigsaw, he said, was still "scattered across the table". Then there was the issue of that IRA text. It was not yet on offer – not yet on the table. Yes, by now, Tony Blair, Jonathan Powell, Bertie Ahern and Michael Collins may well have had some indication of possibilities – but they did not yet have the words of a P O'Neill statement. On Thursday, September 16, Sinn Féin arrived at the castle with the bug under its arms – an offering to "the mighty God of British intelligence". This part played out in public, but then the talking moved inside and we waited for three days from Thursday through to Saturday to see what could be done.

In the build-up, Downing Street was briefing that it was still the intention to get a deal. "We are in a situation where everybody has to take risks," a source told me. "People aren't going to take risks two days before talks, they are going to take risks in the negotiations… These things are always a roller-coaster."

A republican observing the negotiations gave me this assessment: "There's nothing going on there. The expectation is no deal and I wouldn't expect any change. What I'm picking up is they (the DUP) are asking for too much … too much for republicans. My sense of it is that it can't be done. The only caveat offered up (by one of the republican negotiators was)… when Trimble went into the negotiations leading up to the Good Friday Agreement, he didn't want to do a deal and the British Government got him to do it. Can they get Paisley to do a Trimble?"

They were certainly going to try.

MARTIN McGUINNESS: Paisley turned up at Leeds Castle. I have to say I was shocked by his appearance. There were obviously reports prior to Leeds Castle that he wasn't well, that he was receiving treatment… I saw him at very close quarters at Leeds Castle in the dining area where we were all effectively sitting round different tables eating together. And I was really shocked at how weak he looked and how failed he looked, and, to be quite honest, I thought if his state of health continued that he wouldn't have seen out the end of the year. Now, obviously, Leeds Castle was a situation where, if you like for the first time, you had in very close proximity the Democratic Unionist Party, Sinn Féin and the two governments as the key players; others were there, I'm not diminishing their role, but it was obvious that this was the beginning of what we hoped would be a very determined attempt at trying to get a breakthrough, and, obviously, from our perspective, we were intrigued by the possibility that Ian Paisley would sign on for the Good Friday institutions and the Good Friday Agreement albeit protesting and kicking and screaming the whole way along.

Paisley and the DUP were there to negotiate changes to what they call the Belfast Agreement, but, inside the castle, they sensed the governments had other plans – plans to "bounce" them into a deal on the basis of decommissioning and an end to the IRA. On day two of the talks – Friday September 17 – Peter Robinson and his party colleague Nigel Dodds were called out of a meeting with the SDLP and told by Blair's private secretary that the Prime Minister wanted to see them. This meeting, as I understand it, was to explain to the DUP what the governments believed the IRA was prepared to do, or, more accurately, what they thought they could get the IRA to do, but it had another purpose. Robinson and Dodds were told that the governments could not get anybody to agree on the changes that the DUP was seeking to the Agreement. A negotiation on such changes was part of the Leeds Castle agenda, part of the reason why Paisley and his team had turned up and, if this item was now off the agenda, then, the DUP was leaving. Robinson and Dodds consulted their colleagues, including the party leader and, at around midnight, Blair and Ahern got both barrels from Paisley. This was at a British-Irish-DUP meeting, at which the Prime Ministers were joined by their officials, including Jonathan Powell. At the same time, Robinson and Dodds resumed their "adjourned" talks with the SDLP leader Mark Durkan and his colleagues. Back in the room, at that meeting with Blair and the Taoiseach, Paisley stood.

"It was after twelve midnight," he told me when I spoke to him for this book.

PAISLEY: I said to them I'm not sitting down at this meeting, because I'm not having a meeting... I said, I know what you are up to. If the deal is not going through, why not be honest with me and tell me that you fellas have made your deal with the other side (republicans), but, I said, don't try to bluff me.

Going into these talks, the Sinn Féin negotiating team believed an initiative on IRA arms could get Paisley over the line in terms of a deal. The party's chief negotiator Martin McGuinness said this was what they had been told by Blair and Ahern.

McGUINNESS: Prior to going to Leeds Castle, remember we were at Lancaster House (June 2004) and in the immediate aftermath of Lancaster House, and even at our meeting with the Taoiseach and Tony Blair at Lancaster House, we were being told that the only issue that was of major concern to Ian Paisley was the issue of arms. If that could be resolved then Paisley was prepared to go into government with Sinn Féin. So we said: 'Well, OK, we'll have to think about that.' Obviously at a huge disadvantage ourselves; not being able to speak to Ian Paisley because of his unwillingness to speak to us, but we were working in good faith with the Taoiseach and the British Prime Minister, that Paisley's only difficulty was the issue of arms and the resolution of that.

If Blair and Ahern were working on that assumption, then, inside Leeds Castle, at the midnight hour, Paisley was about to put them straight. According to a source, the DUP leader told the prime ministers that he had come to these talks at considerable sacrifice to himself. Paisley had been in hospital, there were concerns about his health, and he had not been able to fly to these negotiations. He had travelled by boat and then by car.

My source said that Blair and Ahern were told that if they believed a deal was possible on the basis of "decommissioning only, without any consideration of changes to structures (the political structures of the Good Friday Agreement)", then "he wasn't interested and the DUP wouldn't be back in the morning".

The intention up until this point had been to run a negotiation right through the night. Indeed, the DUP's transport had been sent away and told it would not be required until six the following morning. But, after the Paisley "stand up", the cars were called back.

"That meeting in its importance will never be overestimated," a party source told me. "It was at that meeting that Blair and Ahern realised that Paisley was interested in a deal."

The source believed this was "a key turning point" in the relationship between Blair and "the Doc".

"The Prime Minister was quite moved. He had underestimated the determination of the Doc in terms of a comprehensive agreement and his will to want to do a deal."

But, inside the room, my source sensed that Powell was uncomfortable and that he was trying to get the door opened to get the DUP out.

"This was not your usual diplomatic meeting," the source told me.

The DUP MEP Jim Allister was also present. I have been told that he spoke frankly to the Prime Minister and told him that if he thought the DUP was at the talks "to take the Belfast Agreement six years on, he was kidding himself". There would be no deal here. The DUP heard a lot about possibilities in terms of what the IRA might do. My source said it was all couched in the language of "I think we can get". I am told that what the British Government thought it could get was a statement from the IRA that it was "going to go away", additional decommissioning witnesses and a photographer to provide that visual proof that the IRA's arms had been put beyond use. But, apparently, when Blair was pushed it became clear that these things were not agreed, but that the government believed they could get republicans to this point. Further down the road, they would get some, but not all, of what they had hoped for. The talks at Leeds Castle broke up without a comprehensive agreement.

PAISLEY: I think they thought that they would collapse me and that I would give something, and then they would run to the other boys (Sinn Féin) and say, well we've got this, let's push a bit further, but it wasn't on.

ROBINSON: I think to some extent Leeds Castle was something that we had to go through, because I think at Leeds Castle both Tony Blair and Bertie Ahern went away convinced about Ian Paisley's bona fides.

ROWAN: In terms of doing a deal?

ROBINSON: Yeah.

ROWAN: The right deal?

ROBINSON: I think before Leeds Castle there had been a lot of nonsense in the papers about divisions in the DUP, that there was a Robinson wing that wanted to do a deal, but a Paisley wing that was resisting, and I think there was a recognition that if it was the right deal, Ian Paisley was willing to sign up to it... Leeds Castle was important, I think, to convince the two prime ministers that Ian Paisley was serious, he wanted to do a deal, but he had very strict limitations within which he would do that deal.

Amid all of the seriousness and the stand-ups and stand-offs at Leeds Castle, there was a funny aside. It happened in the dining room. It was dinner time and Paisley, who is known to be fond of his food, inquired of Sinn Féin's Gerry Kelly what was on the menu. Of course, he didn't know whom he was chatting to. In the darkened dining area he had mistaken the "Shinner" for one of the castle staff. A few of those who were with him, including his son Ian junior, had to put him straight. But when the history of the first exchanges between Paisley and the Provos is written, Leeds Castle may well be revisited. Years earlier, Jim Gibney was the first "Shinner" to shake hands with the British Prime Minister when he put himself at the end of the line as Blair was being introduced to staff at Castle Buildings on the Stormont estate. Now we had this Paisley-Kelly moment. It had nothing to do with politics and everything to do with curry and salad; and, of course, had Paisley recognised Kelly there would have been spoonfuls of stern looks and stony silence on the menu. Paisley junior told me that Kelly was stunned. As for his "da", Ian junior quipped: "His only worry was that he might have been food-poisoned." *Garçon* Kelly, tongue-in-cheek, told me he thought Paisley had been "trying to curry favour", and that maybe he should have offered the Big Man "the green salad starter".

After Leeds Castle the negotiations moved into a phase of what I suppose you could call proximity talks with British and Irish officials shuttling between the DUP and Sinn Féin. On the British side it was Powell, Jonathan Phillips and Robert Hannigan and for the Irish Michael Collins, Brendan Scannell, Tim Dalton and Adrian O'Neill. There was a growing urgency about these talks. A British General Election was likely in May 2005. So, if a deal was to be done and then verified in some "testing period", it would have to be done sooner rather than later. That is why the resources of the two governments and the two main parties were being poured into these negotiations. Days after the Leeds Castle talks, I met two senior members of the DUP for lunch in a restaurant in Holywood. And here, I heard something that suggested to me that the party now knew that whatever else happened, the IRA was not about to formally disband its organisation:

"If the arms are gone, there's no paramilitary activity; if the terrorist structure is away, even if the body is there, it is no longer a paramilitary group. And if they go back (to war), they are in breach of the agreement and we walk away."

This, of course, was all hypothetical – a thinking out loud on what might develop in the negotiations. But that position outlined above is where the IRA moved to in its statement of July 2005 and in acts of decommissioning which followed in September. An end was ordered to the armed campaign but the IRA did not disband. A senior intelligence source described the organisation as being in "hibernation".

Back in September '04, none of this was nailed down and, just a couple of days after that lunch I mentioned a moment ago, one of those senior DUP figures I had met started to express concerns that the government "might be overselling what the Provos might do – not the extent, but the how". My source told me that I could quote him saying "that the issues of decommissioning and paramilitary activity are not yet bolted down. That they (the DUP) still have seen no (IRA) text and have no certainty in these two areas. All they (the DUP) have is the prime minister's version and assessment." In reports for the *BBC News Online* service on September 21 and September 24, I wrote the following:

"The IRA has not yet committed to a text what its contribution might be, but the information jigsaw that is being pieced together suggests an end to all activities and the most significant moves yet on decommissioning. There would be no formal standing down of the IRA but the organisation would leave the stage, it would melt away."

I also said that P O'Neill would speak no more on the political and peace processes. All future republican talking would be left to Sinn Féin, and my reports included a line that the IRA was not planning an "Army Convention".

In the same period, I repeated most of this in a television interview with Noel Thompson, and some who were watching believed that this information had emerged from a formal IRA briefing. It had not, but I knew it was authoritative and that it would stand up when positions were eventually outlined in this negotiation. But, inside republicanism, few would have known the scale of what was being considered. Indeed, on September 22, one long-time source told me he almost "fell off the seat" when he watched that television interview with Thompson.

"I got quite a few phone calls last night about the scale of what was being said," he told me, adding that people "didn't recognise it". What he meant was that people did not believe it. Another republican told me that "things were enormously fraught … around the IRA speculation and around the stuff that you've done". Adams, he said, had complained to the governments about "leaks" – leaks which he said were causing "serious problems".

By now, inside the negotiations, there were draft proposals setting out a timetable towards the restoration of power-sharing in Northern Ireland in early 2005, with decommissioning to be completed by the end of December '04. These were hoped-for positions, and this was another of those negotiations in which nothing was agreed until everything was agreed.

The proximity talks that were about to take place would bring greater clarity to the various positions and, as they approached, the DUP was still pushing for a visual aspect to decommissioning, and, privately, was also stressing the importance of a new witness or witnesses to accompany the de Chastelain team. That the DUP was serious about this negotiation could be seen in its approach to the talks. The party had met the Taoiseach in the Irish Embassy in London as far back as the beginning of 2004, and Paisley and Robinson travelled to Dublin for further talks with Ahern at the end of September. On the eve of those discussions, I had a telephone conversation with Robinson. In the negotiations, the IRA's position was not yet clear. The DUP had not yet seen an IRA text and was "not in a position to make judgements". Robinson told me he believed there was still a problem over the "visual aspect" of decommissioning and the matter of who would accompany de Chastelain.

"I can't see any advantage for them (the IRA) in trying to bluff us (on the extent of what they are prepared to do)," he told me, "(but) they could try to bowl short on the visual aspect and verification. That is one of the reasons we are going South."

After that meeting in Dublin, Paisley said his party was working towards a settlement for all the people of Northern Ireland, and "in so doing we wish to build a relationship with our neighbours that is practically based rather than politically motivated". On the IRA, he said they "must relinquish their guns and be out of business for good… There is no evidence to suggest that there is any IRA offer on the table at the present time."

The republican concern was on other matters, including the changes the government intended to propose around the appointment mechanism for Executive ministers, the issue of ministerial accountability and how the office of First and Deputy First Minister would function. They knew the DUP was not interested in a cosy relationship between Paisley and McGuinness, but anything that looked like the DUP was getting a veto or had the appearance of unionist majority rule was not going to work.

"We haven't seen what they (the government) are up to," a senior republican told me, "and if they are up to no good, then they can fuck off."

In what was going on, the governments were also trying to protect a potentially historic IRA initiative. So there were different focuses and different concerns as those involved in these long talks continued to work to find a way forward.

The reality, of course, was that any IRA offer was always going to be the last minute business of this negotiation or any other negotiation. That is the way the IRA works. Adams and McGuinness would always know the frame within which they could negotiate with the governments and others. They would always be in a position to discuss possibilities and the IRA leadership would always know what they were doing and saying. But "P O'Neill" would only put pen to paper when there was certainty about positions and sequences and this negotiation was not yet there.

Unlike Adams and McGuinness, Paisley and Robinson had not been down this road before. They were not part of the Good Friday Agreement negotiations and all of the subsequent implementation talks. This was the DUP's first time in protracted talks of this kind. What the party knew about the IRA was how to condemn it. But, now, in negotiations through the governments it was trying to put that organisation out of business. The DUP would not have known the complexities of the IRA. It would not have known where the authority of the

Army Council ended and was then passed to a General Army Convention. Many in the party would have had no idea what the IRA constitution said about war and peace and guns. All of this was part of another, unfamiliar, world. A DUP source told me that for some in the party "their knowledge of those complexities grew" as the negotiation became more focused on the issue of weapons and the future of the IRA. But he said there was no doubt that many in the party believed that Adams and McGuinness were "extremely influential" and that their view would prevail. The DUP believed Adams and McGuinness were the IRA, and also believed that they could click their fingers and make that organisation go away. But as this negotiation progressed, there were senior and significant figures in the DUP who began to ask me questions on some of what I have outlined above. They needed to know if Adams and McGuinness could deliver an end to the IRA and how that could be done. In this negotiation, republicans were not looking towards an Army Convention. If it came to making an IRA contribution, then it would be made on leadership orders. But delivering the IRA would only be possible in the context of a comprehensive deal, including a power-sharing Executive at Stormont and agreement on the critical issue of policing.

In the build-up to proximity talks in mid-October, we began to hear some of the things that would need to be said in the context of an overall agreement. The Republic's new foreign minister Dermot Ahern – a senior figure in the Fianna Fail party – said it was only a matter of time before Sinn Féin would be in government both in Dublin and in Belfast. Up to this point, this had not been considered possible in the Republic – but an end to the IRA would open that door.

Also in this period, one of the most senior British military figures, General Sir Mike Jackson, said it was "quite possible" that the normalisation process could begin "this side of Christmas". Normalisation is military speak for pulling down watchtowers, vacating bases and reducing troop numbers. Republicans call it demilitarisation and this was another of their important issues in these talks – so important indeed that, soon, Adams and McGuinness would hold their first ever meeting with the PSNI Chief Constable, Sir Hugh Orde. On the Jackson comments, a senior republican posed the question: Was it a signal that more would be done (on demilitarisation), and quickly?

"The devil is in the detail," he said. "We wait for the small print."

In this period Adams also began to talk out loud about what republicans were willing to do, and said there was "general acceptance" that the IRA was prepared to make "an unprecedented, historic contribution in the context of a comprehensive agreement".

"...It appears to me that there is a certain pandering to the DUP position. Now, I have no problem with the governments exploring the DUP position. The DUP have a mandate and it must be, and should be, respected, and I also know, I'm not stupid, that if the DUP are to come into this process with the rest of us, then there's a certain price to be paid – a certain cost in terms of the rest of us. We have to stretch ourselves, but it cannot be about fundamental issues."

Adams believed an agreement between Sinn Féin, the DUP, the two governments and the other parties was "inevitable", but he said he had yet to discover "the DUP's contribution to achieving this deal".

Ian Paisley junior was also speaking to me throughout these negotiations and, on October 5, he told me that the DUP's problem in trying to assess the IRA's intentions was that "so much of this" was "on the Prime Minister's word". In this type of talking, in negotiations of this kind, the republican hand – and in particular the IRA hand, is always shown last. Long before now, this had become a fact of political life, but, as I mentioned earlier, this was the DUP's first crack at a negotiation of this kind and complexity, and, at times, you could sense a growing impatience. Paisley junior asked me many times for my opinion on the likelihood of the IRA allowing decommissioning to be photographed, and I told him many times that I had heard nothing to suggest that this was possible. I never did, not then in October, not earlier in these negotiations, not later in the talks. There was never a hint from republicans that this could be done. Equally, there was never a suggestion that Paisley's party was prepared to move away from this demand. In a speech during the Conservative Party Conference at Bournemouth, Robinson set out in some detail his party's position within the talks.

"The DUP victory in the Assembly election last November was seen as damaging to the prospects for a political settlement in Northern Ireland by many political commentators and most of the media. I believe they made a fundamental miscalculation. The election transformed the agenda, it gave a greater sense of confidence to the unionist community, it ensured that any agreed settlement would be conclusive and it replaced the tendency to rely on obfuscation and fudge with the need to bring clarity to the critical issues… Reaching a lasting and durable settlement must be valued more highly than getting an early deal cobbled together. That is why the DUP resisted attempts to 'force' a deal at Leeds Castle. A hastily-agreed deal there may have done more harm than good…

"We are clear in what we want to achieve, and that is a fair deal for all of the people of Northern Ireland. Too often the demand for an end to paramilitarism has been characterised as a unionist demand. This has allowed republicans to dress up a fundamental democratic requirement as yet another issue to be traded in negotiations. That must not be allowed to continue…

"On many occasions the failure of the IRA to disarm has been given equivalence with the refusal of unionists to share power with those associated with terrorism. This is absurd. It sends out a dangerous signal and gives an excuse for paramilitaries to hold

onto their guns. Accountability of ministers in an Executive
likewise is a threat to no one. The DUP are not seeking to
introduce these measures to frustrate other parties, but to ensure
that there is a mechanism in place which means the Assembly can
have a say in issues over which there is a legitimate concern. The
DUP would have no interest in blocking progress in an Assembly
to which it has given its consent, and people must remember that
accountability measures will apply equally to DUP ministers as
they will to Sinn Féin or SDLP ministers. Indeed the DUP, with
more ministers in an Executive, would be more subject to these
regulations...

"We are working towards a settlement for all the people of
Northern Ireland and in so doing we wish to build a relationship
with our neighbour that is practically based rather than politically
motivated. No one has anything to fear from an accountable
North-South relationship. If the North-South axis is fashioned to
impel towards a political goal not shared by the people I represent
then a unionist foot will be applied powerfully to the brake.
Nationalists have nothing to gain in those circumstances and
unionists would have everything to fear. If however, shared
practical advantages flow that profit those involved, then my
party will drive co-operation forward with enthusiasm and vigour.
In these circumstances unionists would have nothing to fear and
nationalists would have much to gain from such a relationship.
The talks at Leeds Castle may have ended but the process towards
a settlement in Northern Ireland continues...

"That goal can be achieved with the hard work and genuine
efforts of all those involved. Some may have wanted another
quick fix from 'hot-house' negotiations, but the prize on offer is
much too great to waste on another deadline deal. We are in the
business of delivering a better way forward for the people of
Northern Ireland and we are not about to give up on that."

In another speech six days later, this time in Ballymena,
Robinson's party colleague Jim Allister emphasised the need for a

"testing period" after decommissioning to verify that all IRA activities had ended. This demand was an "immoveable necessity" and was "to ensure Sinn Féin has indeed stepped up to the mark, before there can be any question of a transfer of Executive powers. Words have been found wanting, only verifiable deeds will do." Allister said that "Sinn Féin/IRA" knew what they had to do in terms of destroying their weapons of war, "but to make the transition from terror to democracy they must also irreversibly abandon criminality, including fund-raising by heist". Two months from now, the IRA would be linked to the biggest bank robbery in UK history – just days after this long negotiation failed to produce a deal.

The work of trying to get that deal done continued in the first of the proximity talks which began on October 18. The Sinn Féin negotiating team was based in Hillsborough Castle, the DUP in Jeffrey Donaldson's Lisburn offices and British and Irish officials travelled between the two. Before the talking began, there had been optimistic reports out of Dublin that a deal was "imminent".

The then Secretary of State Paul Murphy added to that mood when, in a speech in Chepstow, he said that within the next two weeks he believed there was an opportunity for both sides to take "dramatic, decisive and unequivocal steps forward which themselves will form the basis of a new relationship". On the same day – October 18 – Martin McGuinness said Sinn Féin had "grave concerns" about government proposals on the political institutions, and, late the following night, Tuesday, October 19, I was given this private republican assessment of the proximity talks: "I think we are further away (from a deal) than we were yesterday. Maybe the last few days have helped clarify the problems and clarify just how difficult it is going to be to resolve them... Without getting involved in (a discussion on) how we got to today, today wasn't a good day, yesterday wasn't a good day. The problem is at the door of the DUP."

On that "problem" with the DUP, he said he wasn't sure

whether it was "wobbles, tactical or factions".

"It could be the DUP in its first negotiation finding it's not all it's cracked up to be."

The following day, this same source added the following: "If the positions we have are what they (the DUP) are sticking with, then we are going nowhere."

In this phase of the negotiation, during those Hillsborough-Lisburn talks, Jonathan Powell, it is said, somewhat reluctantly passed a Sinn Féin position paper to the DUP.

"It was a terrible letter," Ian Paisley told me, "one of the most stinking letters ever."

Another senior DUP figure, recalling that moment, said: "I think that the government recognised that the tone of the document was such that it would not be conducive to people wanting to proceed, didn't want to read it, but were forced to do so, didn't want to hand it over, but were forced to do so, and it got a steamy reply."

Ian Paisley told me his party had responded with "full pelt". Sinn Féin had clearly wound up the DUP and that party had responded in kind, but this was shadow boxing. This negotiation was not yet down into its closing and critical moments, and neither side had yet fully expressed its bottom line. The republican mood, at this time, was that the talking was stuck. Indeed, one source believed the talks would be closed down and that another effort to achieve a deal would be made some time in the following year, but he also made this observation:

"The DUP are in the negotiating arena and they aren't going to get out of it. It's when (there will be a deal), not if."

Adams was clearly annoyed that, in the period around the proximity talks, there was the Dublin and Murphy commentary pointing to a possible short-term breakthrough, and he put his thoughts on paper for the New York based *Irish Voice* newspaper.

"I have to say that such remarks always irritate me, and I always wonder why they are made," Adams wrote. "Perhaps it's no more than the compulsion of politicians to be positive. Perhaps it is a political instinct to have fingerprints on a process just in case there is a breakthrough. Whatever the reason, when you hear such off-the-cuff comments from either of the two governments, take it with a pinch of salt. Of course, a breakthrough is possible. That's what we are working for and it will happen, but better to wait until it is actually achieved before flagging it up."

In this article Adams also restated that the IRA would only move in the context of an overall agreement. He acknowledged that there had been positive signals from the DUP. The party had said it was for power-sharing and Paisley had gone to Dublin and had stated publicly his desire to build "good neighbourliness". But, a month after the Leeds Castle talks, Adams said the negotiation was no further on.

"If the governments are satisfied with what they have proclaimed the IRA is going to do, then who are they waiting on? Obviously (it is) the DUP."

Adams said Ian Paisley's party still had a mountain to climb, and he posed the question:

"How long must we wait for the DUP to come into the real world?"

Coming out of the Hillsborough-Lisburn talks, republicans did not sense that the governments would try to "bounce" the DUP, and one source remarked that if a deal had to wait until "post-election" – the expected British General Election of May 2005 – then it would be "post-post-election".

His political crystal ball had shown him a clear picture. Events would be in line with that conclusion and the business of deal-making would have to wait not only until after the election, but until after the IRA had moved unilaterally on the question of its activities and the issue of arms.

In that period of late 2004, the talking continued for several more weeks. At different times there were moments of optimism, but this particular phase of negotiation would end, not in breakthrough, but in breakdown. After the first of the proximity talks, a senior DUP source told me that "very considerable progress" had been made since the discussions at Leeds Castle. He meant there was now more certainty about the IRA would do, which he believed had been oversold by the governments at the talks in Kent those few weeks earlier; oversold in the sense that things had not been nailed down at that stage. My source told me he was finding this process of negotiation "agonisingly slow", but he did not believe it had arrived at the point of an "insurmountable obstacle". That obstacle would prove to be the demand for visual proof of decommissioning. Just days after the "considerable progress" assessment, the DUP and Sinn Féin were having a public sword fence. In a radio interview on October 23, Mitchel McLaughlin dismissed visual decommissioning as "a humiliating scenario that simply isn't going to happen". It was a comment that was consistent with everything republicans had been telling me. As I mentioned earlier, there was never, in any conversation I had, any suggestion that decommissioning photographs would be offered up to the DUP. But, in a few weeks time, I would find out why that party believed it was possible, and why with some there was a growing confidence about this right up to the point of this negotiation breaking down.

Peter Robinson responded to McLaughlin's comments by repeating that there "must be a visual aspect to the decommissioning of IRA weaponry".

"Sinn Féin/IRA is at the forefront of demands to have security installations dismantled in a very public way with the world's press and media being present. Crown forces and the unionist community have been humiliated by the way in which bases and stations have been demolished and by the treatment of those who have defended our Province."

He accused Sinn Féin of attempting "to develop an exit strategy from the process". There would be another go at proximity talks in London in late October, but this issue of decommissioning, and how the DUP wanted it done, kept coming back again and again. Paisley said there would be "no fudge" – "no compromise".

"It must be totally transparent and visible to the people whose lives are threatened by these weapons."

Significant progress was being made within the negotiations, including progress on decommissioning. This was something I discovered during a meeting on November 13. I will call it the "Kina conversation" because of where it took place – in a café in Holywood's High Street. At the time I was working on a television documentary for the BBC *Spotlight* programme, and this was part of my research.

By now, I had already recorded interviews with Peter Robinson, Mitchel McLaughlin, Chief Constable Sir Hugh Orde and the then Army GOC Sir Phillip Trousdell. The documentary was an attempt to piece together the negotiations and to assess the prospects for a deal. At this point, the government was also trying to fit the loyalist pieces into the jigsaw. There had been meetings with senior political and paramilitary figures from that community. In one of those meetings, the then Secretary of State Paul Murphy met the Ulster Defence Association "brigadiers" Jackie McDonald, Andre Shoukri and Billy McFarland. This was all part of a sequence of events leading to the Northern Ireland Office "de-specifying" the UDA, meaning it again recognised its ceasefire. Part of the choreography was another statement from the paramilitary group.

This was read at its "Remembrance Day" parades on Sunday, November 14. There had been some expectation that the paramilitary leadership would announce that it was standing down its organisation, but its final words failed to live up to that billing and they were always going to. Such an outcome could not be delivered within the ranks of the largest of the loyalist paramilitary groups. In the end, the organisation committed itself "to work towards a day when there is no longer a need for a UDA and a UFF (the linked Ulster Freedom Fighters)".

"We have agreed with our government to enter into a process which will see the eradication of all paramilitary activity. We will engage with the decommissioning commission, though we must be satisfied there is no longer any threat to our community from without or within. Furthermore, we need to be certain that this latest attempt to find a political settlement is for real."

The biggest threat to the loyalist community was then, and is now, an internal one, and the biggest question, even after this statement, continued to be: Is the UDA for real? These are issues I will deal with in greater detail later. Back in November 2004, the government's approach to these talks was about trying to re-involve loyalists in the peace process, and to ensure that if a deal was done, that no one would be left behind. By mid-November there was again some optimism that the talks might deliver such a deal, and there was the first look inside the door of these negotiations.

The "Kina conversation" gave me an insight into new proposals on decommissioning and what the governments were still trying to achieve. My source told me there was still no agreement on photographs, but the governments were trying to re-open a discussion with Adams and McGuinness along the following lines:

- Could photographs be taken?
- Could they be published?
- If not, who would see them and when?

My source posed the question: "Is there any creative way of doing it?"

This was what the governments were still trying to explore, and a scenario based on the above would be seen in their proposals for a comprehensive agreement when they were eventually published on December 8.

Outside the café came the big news of this conversation. My source disclosed that there was now "agreement in principle" for two churchmen to witness the decommissioning and, in later conversations, he told me this was "PAC (Provisional Army Council) agreed."

I also learned that there was now a republican text in the negotiation – the words that could become the P O'Neill statement in the event of a deal being reached. This first text was read to the DUP by Jonathan Powell during those proximity talks in mid-October when British and Irish officials were travelling between Lisburn and Hillsborough.

"One of the interesting comments made during that meeting was by (the Irish official) Tim Dalton, who said what the British and Irish governments were seeking here was a settlement and not a transitional deal," a DUP source told me. "That was the first time that word 'settlement' was used."

The text, and now the news of the witnesses, was the evidence of the considerable progress that had been made since Leeds Castle.

"If the transparency issue (on decommissioning) could be sorted out, it would be a spectacular deal," the source I met at Café Kina told me.

He said there would be no inventory on decommissioning until the entire process was completed. That meant loyalist guns as well, but, as a first step, "de Chastelain needs to be able to say he has overseen the decommissioning of all IRA weapons". This is what we would hear him say in September 2005, at a time when loyalist guns had been all too loud in feuding and in attacks on the security forces. The *Spotlight* documentary was scheduled for Tuesday November 16, just three days after the "Kina conversation". Immediately I left the café, I spoke to the programme producer Elaine Forrester and told her we now needed to build a story around the witnesses and the fact that there was now a republican text in the negotiations. On the eve of the programme, I met a republican source in Andersonstown in west Belfast. I wanted to discuss the issue of photographs, and I was told that I could "understand" that republicans viewed "any visual aspect as humiliation and therefore unacceptable". I told my source what I intended to report the following day on witnesses and the republican text. He would not confirm the information I had, but said it was "enough to scare the hell out of people". The detail of this negotiation was being kept within a very tight group of republicans, and across the IRA organisation there would be no knowledge of this proposal to introduce new church witnesses, and the fact that in the context of an overall agreement, the Army Council had agreed to this.

From that meeting in west Belfast, I then travelled to the home of the Reverend Ken Newell, who at that time was the Moderator of the Presbyterian Church in Ireland. I had arranged for Elaine Forrester and a camera crew to meet me there. In talks with republicans back in the early 90s, Newell had sensed the first moves towards some conflict resolution process. But it would take years for what he calls the "frozen mantras" to thaw.

NEWELL: I felt as I said at the time that I was talking to an answering machine, which was always getting the same answer: Brits have to go before the IRA stops the violence, and the same with the loyalists: We will never stop our campaign against republicans until they declare that there is a ceasefire. It was very, very predictable. They were what I call frozen mantras, and a year and a half into the dialogue, I honestly felt that I understood the soul of republicanism and we were going nowhere, because the deepest agenda of their soul was not peace. It was justifying the armed struggle... I therefore pulled out and over the summer with (the Clonard priests) Al Reid and Gerry Reynolds went and talked to the folk who'd asked them (republicans) to bring us into the dialogue; and basically they said to the leadership of the Republican movement that we were talking with: If you can't connect with the Protestants who've been talking with you in Clonard for a year and a half, you'll never connect with the unionist population. And I think that took time to sink in, but that thought was parachuted into their mind, it was left over the summer, and when we were asked to come back in, we said we would only go back in if we talked about conflict resolution.

Conflict resolution has been the business of this process since the ceasefires of 1994, and ten years on from then, we were at the point of an initiative that would remove the threat of the IRA's guns. In confidence, I told Newell the story of the witnesses and also told him that there was still no agreement on decommissioning photographs. He has been around this process long enough to recognise that progress was being made and he told me that if it came down to a choice, he would rather have "talking eyes" than "silent photographs".

"These have to be people who are trusted. These must be people whose word is their bond, and people who are against any kind of exaggeration or hype, because people today have a great scepticism about the whole spinning industry that's there. They want people to speak the truth, to tell it as it is and to talk straight. And, if they can get that, then I think you're going to see trust building up."

Newell is a long-time friend of Father Alex Reid, one of the churchmen who would eventually witness the decommissioning process in September 2005. In an interview for this book, recorded in October 2005, I asked the former Moderator why he had argued for those "talking eyes" rather than the Paisley demanded photographs.

NEWELL: Well, first of all because I realised that the photographs were not going to be acceptable to republicans and to the leadership of Sinn Féin, that that was being seen as a humiliation. Also I wasn't a hundred percent sure how far the demand for photographs – how deep that was within the DUP itself. I knew there were people who were articulating that, but I wasn't sure how much conviction there was behind that. And, therefore, I took the line that while photographs would have been beneficial they were not essential. I really took that line in order to say to people: OK, you are not going to get photographs, but don't hang everything on photographs. You're not going to get them. They would have had certain benefits like building confidence and trust. They would have given you (the DUP) a sense that what you asked for was also part of the ingredients in the final act of decommissioning; but, basically, look for an alternative approach.

The DUP was very nervous when I told them that I was about to run the story on the witnesses and wanted it stressed that the party was not responsible for the leak. It was not, but I knew this was a story that stood up and stood out. At six o'clock the following evening – a few hours before the *Spotlight* programme – the BBC ran this report across its output:

"This is a significant move by republicans, but it's still not clear whether it will be enough for the DUP. They've been demanding more visibility around decommissioning. In the event of a comprehensive deal, republicans have now agreed that two churchmen – one from each side of the community – could witness the IRA put its weapons beyond use.

"There's no agreement yet on who they'll be. All of this has been discussed inside the political negotiations and not in direct talks between the IRA and General de Chastelain. Inside those negotiations, efforts are still being made to secure photographic evidence of decommissioning. The governments want to discuss possibilities:

"Could photographs be taken?

"Could they be published?

"Or, could they be shown privately to those who need to be convinced?

"Up to this point, republicans have said no. In recent weeks, the DUP have been saying that progress has been made since the Leeds Castle talks. The agreement on church witnesses confirms this."

To put it mildly, Adams was not happy that the story of the churchmen and other details of the negotiations had got out. His party complained to the Irish Government, but Sinn Féin could not identify the source of the leak. The following morning on radio, David Trimble suggested that the story had emerged from a republican briefing, something I dismissed on the same programme as "complete and utter nonsense". Later that day, a senior republican told me that my reports had "caused enormous problems and annoyed an enormous number of people". In this conversation, he made the point that Adams and McGuinness were "at the coalface, not just of the negotiations, but management (the internal republican management of this process)". He told me the *Spotlight* report had caused "considerable angst". This takes us back to the point that these negotiations were being handled by a very small group of republicans, and detailed knowledge did not extend beyond that inner cabinet.

The day after the *Spotlight* programme – November 17 – at separate meetings in Dublin and London, Sinn Féin and the DUP were given the governments' proposals for a comprehensive agreement. The negotiation was now in its most critical phase and it was getting closer to decision time. Twenty four hours later, in an initial response, Ian Paisley issued the following statement.

"I took possession from the prime minister of government proposals aimed at resolving outstanding issues and forming a comprehensive agreement. Over the next few days we shall continue to study the paper and consult within the party on its contents. Initial scrutiny shows that there are some areas of confusing ambiguity and even apparent inconsistency. We will also want to have clarification on a number of matters where there is a lack of detail or the use of imprecise text. While on one construction it is possible, if our outstanding concerns were removed, to see a basis for agreement, other interpretations of some sections would result in a less favourable judgement. We must not allow a lack of clarity to lead to misunderstanding and dispute at a later stage. We will need the prime minister to confirm to us that in each and every respect the IRA has accepted the nature, extent and particulars of that part of the agreement which impacts on its activities and position. The DUP still sees improvements which are possible and at least one important issue which is not addressed by the proposals.

"We shall engage positively with the government over the coming days in an effort to resolve outstanding matters and gain essential clarification and progress on remaining issues of concern."

Over the next few days, in conversations with some senior DUP figures, I got the impression that they were becoming increasingly confident on the issue of photographs. On November 21, one party source gave me this assessment:

"They (republicans) are not going to go for the final OK for that unless they are sure we are signing on to (the) politics. That (agreement on decommissioning photographs) will be the eleventh hour and 59th minute."

The following day I spoke to Peter Robinson at the party's offices in east Belfast. He told me that photographs were "an essential aid" in terms of confidence on decommissioning, and he was adamant "there won't be a deal without them". Robinson seemed confident, and jokingly asked me would I be prepared to wager £100. I said, I didn't think he was a betting man. He said, he wasn't, but he liked to invest. It was all a bit of banter – nothing more than that – but he was so confident, that the following day, I made another check at the republican end. The line here was consistent with everything I had heard previously. My source had "heard nothing to suggest this was within the realms of possibility". So why was Robinson, and why were others in the DUP, so confident that this could be done. I spoke to the DUP deputy leader in October 2005.

ROWAN: When did Powell or Phillips or whoever it was or Blair tell you definitively: We can't get you the photographs?

ROBINSON: Well they didn't. They always indicated that they were having difficulty with the issue of photographs. The issue of photographs was not whether there would be photographs, but whether the photographs would be published in December (2004) or March (2005). I would have to say that there was a slight difference within our group. Ian wanted them published upfront in December. I preferred it in March. I preferred it in March because I knew there was going to be an election shortly afterwards and I wanted a fresh memory for people at that time...

ROWAN: So, as far as you were concerned the only issue about photographs was the publication date?

ROBINSON: The publication date, December or March.

ROWAN: The governments were basically saying or indicating that they had this sorted?

ROBINSON: There was no indication to us that they can't get photographs or wouldn't be able to get photographs.

On November 24, the DUP and Sinn Féin held separate talks in London with Blair and Ahern, and twenty-four hours later, I got a detailed read-out on the timetable and events that the governments hoped would lead to the restoration of devolution in Northern Ireland and a new power-sharing Executive – an Executive that if established would have Ian Paisley and Martin McGuinness as First and Deputy First Ministers. The information emerged in a meeting at three o'clock on the afternoon of Thursday, November 25. My source had read the proposals put forward by both governments and, in my reporting, I described him as a talks insider. He told me the paper was "specific in terms of photographs being taken and published and de Chastelain holding them for a certain period of time". This would be until the day of devolution. He told me: "Everyone is aware, no publication means no deal." The church witnesses would be present at "all" acts of decommissioning:

"It makes it clear the witnesses see the photographs being taken. The paper is clear cut on these issues."

He told me Paisley was "likely" to see the photographs before publication, and my source said that de Chastelain's final report on IRA decommissioning "will come before the end of the year, probably before Christmas. We are told it's physically possible."

In terms of devolution, the target date being worked on was March 2005, and in the governments' proposals, there was a plan for a shadow Assembly to be in place by January.

"That's all part of the roll-out," my source said.

This was the plan in its finest detail. My source was not suggesting that the IRA had agreed to everything that was in the document. These were the governments' proposals, but I now had the picture that was in the heads of Blair and Ahern – their vision of the comprehensive agreement. After my meeting, I spoke to Adams' aide Richard McAuley and to Downing Street. McAuley was furious. He told me that somebody was "seriously fucking around".

"It's deeply dangerous, its 'fuckology'. That's bad stuff," he told me.

He called me back to say that Adams was going "ballistic" and that he was "very pissed off". McAuley did not comment on the accuracy or otherwise of the information I had, and the Downing Street spokesman also refused to discuss the details. He said, "Only a very few people know the whole picture", and that "speculation that depends on any one source is probably that".

The publication of the proposals on December 8 would confirm that my source was one of the "very few" who knew the "whole picture". On the morning of November 26, I ran the following report:

"More details are emerging on proposals from the governments to deal with the demand for visible decommissioning. Talks insiders suggest that by the end of December, General de Chastelain could report that all IRA weapons have been put beyond use. Photographic proof of decommissioning would be held by him until March, when there would be a new power-sharing Executive.

"Talks sources say the proposals from the two governments are very clear. If a deal is done, then by the end of this year – just six weeks away – General de Chastelain would report that all IRA weapons have been put beyond use. This would open the door to a shadow Assembly at the start of January.

"Two churchmen, agreed by the DUP and republicans, would witness the acts of decommissioning. And sources say under the governments' proposals, photographs would be taken, but would not be published immediately. General de Chastelain would hold the pictures until March, the latest target date for devolution to be restored. This is when the DUP and Sinn Féin would enter a new power-sharing Executive. We don't yet know how much of this the parties will agree to, but the DUP is saying without photographs there will be no deal.

"That said there's nothing coming from republicans at this time to suggest that the IRA has agreed to this proposal."

On the details revealed in my report, here is precisely what was proposed in the comprehensive agreement when it was published on December 8.

DECEMBER

IICD (Independent International Commission on Decommissioning) announces commencement of decommissioning process.

IICD report confirms 100% (end month) of IRA arms decommissioned.

JANUARY
Shadow Assembly established.

MARCH
First Minister/Deputy First Minister confirmed by the Assembly.

In annex D of the document there were proposed elements for an IICD statement, including the following:

"The IRA representative has indicated that in response to our request to agree mechanisms which would enhance public confidence in the decommissioning process, additional arrangements will be put in place. These will include the presence as observers during the process of two clergymen nominated by the two governments following appropriate consultation... In addition the IRA representative has told us that the IRA will have photographs of the weapons and *materiel* involved taken by the IICD, in the presence of the independent observers.

"These photographs will be shown by the IICD to the two governments and the parties at the time of the final report on IRA decommissioning and will be published at the time the Executive is established."

These proposals were entirely consistent with what my source had told me in that meeting on November 25, and with what I reported the following morning. And it is clear that the concern among republicans and in Downing Street was that what I had was too accurate. The concern was that it was about to be aired publicly while crucial final discussions were taking place and before the planned publication of the document on the comprehensive agreement. At that meeting on November 25, I had been given a look inside the treasure chest of this negotiation. You can see in that document I have outlined why the DUP was becoming increasingly confident on the issue of photographs. The problem, however, was that these were proposals from the governments – written in that context – and not agreed by the IRA.

There had been no discussion between the organisation's representative and de Chastelain on the issue of photographs. But this document – compiled by the governments – gave an impression that this could be delivered, and, as I mentioned earlier, there were those in the DUP who believed the IRA would buy into this in that 59th minute of the eleventh hour. Why else would such proposals be written into such a document?

ROWAN: Did you ever directly ask the IRA were photographs possible, or did you just have enough common sense to realise that there was no point?

MARTIN McGUINNESS: I did ask them, and if the IRA had said yes, I would have said hurrah, but it was obvious, I think, to the IRA that Paisley wanted the photographs, probably more to use against David Trimble, but also to use against the IRA, because the governments and civil servants at different levels didn't hide the prospect that if any photographs emerged, that they would be on every lamp post on the streets of Belfast on the run in to the Westminster elections. So, the two governments were told that I had broached the issue of photographs and the IRA had said no. So, for them then to have gone on and given Ian Paisley the prospect that there would be photographs was folly of the worst kind.

The government had also given the DUP a clarification document on November 25, which republicans knew nothing about. I was told of the existence of this document on December 9, 24 four hours after the collapse of this long negotiation. It was read to me by a member of the DUP:

"…The Commission (IICD) would be augmented by former commissioner Tauno Nieminen, an experienced photographer who could be authorised to take the photographs. It is not possible to specify the numbers of photographs, but the IICD will satisfy itself that the photographs will represent accurate and persuasive indicators of the weapons and *materiel* involved. The independent observers will also be present at the taking of the photographs."

This was one of around forty pieces of clarification sought by the DUP after it had received the original proposals from the government on November 17. When I learned of the document, I called Richard McAuley for a Sinn Féin comment. The party had not seen this document. Adams contacted Jonathan Powell and, afterwards, a Downing Street spokesman, called me:

"So as there is no misunderstanding, at all stages, this was always regarded as proposals... we are not accusing anyone of bad faith."

The DUP source who read the document to me summed his thoughts up with this comment:

"The assumption I make (is) all we ever got from Blair was a gut feeling. He never tied the other side down."

The party leader Ian Paisley shared that view.

PAISLEY: The Prime Minister, in my opinion, thinks he has got what he thinks he should be getting. And he made up his mind he needs to get so much (from) the IRA, and he thought he had it.

Martin McGuinness told me the governments had pursued this whole concept of a photograph against republican advice. He said it had been made "crystal clear" to them that the IRA would be "totally hostile" to it, and he said it was "a mistake" for the governments to have included it in their proposals. On that document given to the DUP on November 25 which suggested Tauno Nieminen as a photographer, he said his party had never seen "any such text". In October 2005, I spoke to Martin McGuinness for this book.

McGUINNESS: I think that most people at the heart of the negotiations actually accepted that it was much better to have witnesses than have photographs, but Paisley majored on the issue of photographs.

ROWAN: Because he was being told he could get them?

McGUINNESS: Well, I don't know if he was being told he could get them.

ROWAN: Well I read a document where he was told that Tauno Nieminen could be the photographer and while we can't tell you how many photographs, it will be persuasive in terms of what was delivered. That raised in their minds the possibility that this could be done.

McGUINNESS: Yeah, on one hand it raised in their minds the possibility that it could be done vis-à-vis Tauno Nieminen, his name being mentioned, the fact that he was out of it (no longer a member of the IICD) indicated that he was going to be brought back into it, but we, absolutely right throughout the whole course of 2004, told the two governments that it was our sense of it, and we had a good sense of it, that the photographic dimension of this was a total and absolute non-runner... Whatever notions the DUP harboured about getting a photographic dimension, they could not have been, under any circumstances, under the illusion that that was something that could be delivered from the republican side. I would have been very surprised if the two governments weren't saying to Ian Paisley that Gerry Adams and I had told them that the IRA would be very hostile to that dimension. So, maybe that was injected as a means of bringing Paisley along... Maybe the British did harbour the notion that if things came to a big deal that at some stage Gerry Adams and I could go back to the IRA and get a photographic dimension, but never at any stage did we give either of the governments any succour, for want of a better word, on the issue of a photographic dimension, for the simple reason, when we asked the IRA about the issue, we were told very clearly it was a non-runner...

On September 28, 2005, I asked General de Chastelain about the issue of photographs. He told me that his Commission had "requested that Nieminen come back", and "that if there were photographs to be taken, he could do it". But de Chastelain knew the IRA's position on this: "They told us before there would be no photographs."

In the days just before the final collapse of this negotiation on December 8, there had been a number of significant moments – a thunderous speech from Paisley which shook the whole process from top to bottom, and, then, a first-ever meeting between the Sinn Féin leadership and the PSNI Chief Constable Sir Hugh Orde. On the evening of Friday November 26, Ian Paisley junior called me. At the time, I was pushing a shopping trolley round the supermarket. He told me his father was speaking at a dinner in Kells – near Ballymena – the following evening. He was addressing the party's North Antrim Association, and Bill Lowry, the former head of Special Branch in Belfast, would also be speaking. Paisley junior suggested I might want to send a camera along, but he did not tell me what his father was going to say. This was not the type of event that television cameras would normally be invited to, but it would turn out to be a key moment in the period of these talks. I called the BBC on Friday evening and arrangements were made to be there. John Crawford was the only cameraman at the dinner when Paisley spoke his words.

Other key figures in the DUP only learned of the planned speech on Saturday, and, hours later, the party leader was in full flow and at his most biting.

"The IRA needs to be humiliated and they need to wear their sackcloth and ashes not in a backroom but openly, and we have no apology for the stand we are taking."

These words did not destroy the possibility of decommissioning photographs. There had been no suggestion from republicans that the IRA was going to deliver this visual proof, and, at no time in this negotiation, had there ever been a film in the cameras of the IRA or the IICD. But what this speech did do was confirm in the republican mind the purpose behind the demand.

They believed that Paisley had let the decommissioning cat out of the humiliation bag. As far as republicans were concerned, the photographs were not about confidence building, they were about something else, and the DUP leader had said it loud and clear.

But why was the camera at the Kells dinner? What was the motivation behind the Paisley junior invite? There was a view at the time that this had been a deliberate attempt to wreck the prospects for a deal. Paisley junior denies this. In an interview for this book, recorded on October 10 2005, he said the purpose of the invite was to "get on-the-record a particular party line, and a leader line, at a time whenever the negotiations and the whole political process were at a crucial point". He said his father had delivered that line "in his own inimitable style".

ROWAN: People said at the time, this was you on a solo run; this was you attempting to wreck the process.

PAISLEY JUNIOR: I wish I'd that power. I don't have that authority, I don't have that power, and my father is too long in the political game to be used like that. He ain't the puppet in anything, and I'm not the string master in anything, and I think that is just codswallop to be honest with you. We'd discussed at length, he'd discussed at length, how he wanted to sell this particular message and get that message out loud and clear, and that's exactly what happened, and it was in line, and it was exactly in line, with our negotiation strategy... For about four months we'd used the terminology internally, there has to be a sincerity test, the sincerity of the Provisionals has to be tested and we tried that in different ways, and it was pretty clear to us that they had failed the sincerity test, and put it like this, a few tough words from the "Big Man" of unionism wasn't really going to hurt the great Oglaigh na hEireann...

ROWAN: Did you believe that weekend that the photographs issue was dead?

PAISLEY JUNIOR: Yip.

ROWAN: Before your father spoke?

PAISLEY JUNIOR: It died two weeks before that, probably even longer than that. All along I'd taken the view, that we should have asked for things that were reasonable, and let's test their sincerity. Could they deliver? It was not unreasonable to ask for photographs given what unionism had to visually go through. However, I never believed that the Provisional movement would ever deliver on that... The Provisionals were never mentally there to see their game over, and visually their game would be seen to be over if they delivered on photographs.

ROWAN: Some people thought this was your father on the doorstep, if you like, of a deal with the Provos, and running away at the last minute – that he never wanted to do business with those people.

PAISLEY JUNIOR: Some people not so far away from me – (the author) – described it as the "deal of all deals", the "unthinkable". Well we've taken the view, and he's taken the view that it would stick in his craw having to do a particular deal, or make a particular arrangement, go into a particular government with particular people. So, I don't believe he was found wanting in any of that. The people who were found wanting, the Provisionals, couldn't match what I have described in the past as their waffle, their words, with the reality of what democracy demands. They always want more than they are entitled to, and they always wanted to have their cake and eat it, and we were just demonstrating that if you want democracy this is the door you have to walk through, you have to convince us, we're the people who are not convinced by your sincerity, cross our sincerity test threshold and then you'll see how generous we actually can be. We were sincere in all of that... I'll tell you who did believe that we were sincere, the

British Government believed we were sincere, the Irish Prime Minister believed we were sincere: others knew that we were sincere because we were taking a massive risk in all of this. It was the IRA who fell short at the end of the day, not us.

MARTIN McGUINNESS: Whenever we get involved in negotiations we do an awful lot of work and it's not just around what's going on at the heart of the negotiations. It's very important to find out where different people are at, particularly the different influences who are around the key players, and a big influence around Ian Paisley is his family, and it is clear to me that there is a huge hostility within the Paisley family to Ian Paisley signing up for the Good Friday Agreement.

ROWAN: Do you think the family had more influence on Paisley in that negotiation than Robinson and those around Robinson?

McGUINNESS: Absolutely. I don't think there's any doubt about it whatsoever, and I think the two key players in Ian Paisley's life are his wife Eileen and his son Ian Paisley junior, politically speaking… We are dealing with someone, who for whatever reason stood up in Ballymena and demanded sackcloth and ashes, and of course we say to ourselves: 'Well what's that all about?' … And it certainly fits into the sense that I have that these other influences in Ian Paisley's life can become predominant at critical times in the process… I have no doubt about it that that (the Ballymena speech) was Ian Paisley junior's baby. The fact that the former head of the Special Branch stood up at the same meeting and castigated the Sinn Féin leadership, and then some days later said different things about where he thought Gerry Adams and I were coming from, but it just showed that there was something going on around Paisley which was about trying to scuttle the prospect of an agreement, and I think that was what Ballymena was all about.

The talking and the business of trying to make a deal continued for days after the Paisley speech, and, on Sunday, November 28, the story broke that there would be a Blair-Orde-Sinn Féin meeting in Downing Street the following day. Sinn Féin said it was about demilitarisation, but Orde said he wanted to talk about policing. I subsquently asked the Chief Constable did he see this as a public signal that republicans were ending their cold war, if you like, with the police; that here we had the first meeting between Adams, McGuinness and a Northern Ireland Chief Constable.

"It was important, it was symbolic in that sense," he told me, "but as everybody knows, and I say ad nauseam, the notion that they (Sinn Féin) weren't talking (to the police) is barking. So if formalising the reality helped, it may have moved us a step in the right direction."

ORDE: The interesting thing was that the meeting took place. It was not secret. It was known that it was going to happen. It wasn't an event that was behind the scenes. That was sensible, because it was never going to be kept behind the scenes, and my purpose was very clear. It was to talk about policing. They needed the top cover of demilitarisation, which was a bit of a charade, because they knew about demilitarisation... I told them we had delivered against Patten (the Patten Report on police reforms)... (and) the only thing that was stopping us becoming more effective was their unwillingness to join policing. That's what I said, and they talked about demilitarisation, but that was very straightforward, because demilitarisation was dependent on a number of other things that were outside my gift.

The government had already prepared a demilitarisation plan which was ready to roll out as a response to the IRA ending all activities and completing the decommissioning process.

The organising of Monday's Downing Street meeting was very much the stuff of the last minute.

"It did unfold rather quickly," Orde told me. He was out for a Sunday walk with friends along a coastal path when he got the call to go to London. At home, his son booked his flights and his hotel over the internet, and in London on Sunday night Orde contacted his assistant chief constable Peter Sheridan and asked him to travel first thing the following morning. The Downing Street meeting was round the table in the Cabinet Room. Orde was accompanied by Sheridan and his director of media and public relations, Sinead McSweeney. Tony Blair was there, Jonathan Powell and the Northern Ireland Office officials Jonathan Phillips, Robert Hannigan with Nick Perry, the director of security policy. Adams, McGuinness and Gerry Kelly represented Sinn Féin.

"I told them success for me was a civilian police service in a civilian society and I knew what my responsibilities were in relation to that. My challenge to them was: What are yours?" Orde said to me later.

He told me he knew that using "mediaeval towers to deliver 21st century policing" wasn't very good, but he needed republicans to help create the environment in which the army watchtowers in south Armagh could be pulled down and the police could operate without military support. Already they were driving along roads that they hadn't travelled for many, many years. In that meeting in November 2004, Orde knew what he was dealing with. It was "leap of faith stuff, Catch 22, who jumps first?"

"I did make the point, if they didn't come onboard soon there would be nothing left for them to barter with, because we would have done what we needed to do just on the basis of good policing and local decision-making."

Orde got no sense that on the policing question there was any "real energy" on the republican side to move more quickly.

"I just got the impression that these people would move at the speed that suited them to maximise their benefit... I think they knew we were good, I also think they thought a lot of policing was good. What I couldn't form a clear view on was how far advanced they were in discussions with their communities as to how they engage in policing in a more formal sense."

Across the table, Orde heard this was "hard" for republicans. He said the impression he formed was that they "were doing victim", but he told me: "I don't do sympathy very well."

Endorsing policing in the context of a partitionist state will arguably be the most significant and difficult republican decision in this process. In November 2004 the groundwork had not been prepared.

And, in Downing Street, all republicans wanted to hear from Orde was that in the event of a deal, demilitarisation would happen and happen more quickly than the timeframe envisaged in the government plan.

As that meeting in Number 10 broke up, Orde's colleague Peter Sheridan complimented Martin McGuinness on his mother's "lovely soup", but he didn't tell him how he knew. Sheridan had had it served up to him two days earlier on a tray decorated with a doiley. He had been in the Bogside on the Saturday at the home of the writer and commentator Nell McCafferty. He wanted her to sign a copy of her book and had planned on staying about 15 seconds, but his visit lasted something closer to four hours. Nell introduced the "top cop" to her elderly "mammy" and, as they chatted, Sheridan was given a screwdriver to mend a broken bell-push. Then came Peggy McGuinness' soup. Nell served him up a bowl with a couple of slices of bread before telling him who had made it. It was so good that Sheridan felt the need to compliment the chef, and on the back of his police business card he wrote the words, "Peggy, wonderful soup". He left it with Nell to give to McGuinness' mother. Peggy would later relate the story to Martin, but the "Shinner" had not yet been told when Sheridan spoke to him at the close of that meeting in the Cabinet Room.

Paisley was back in Downing Street the following day for yet another meeting with Blair, and outside afterwards, he repeated his comments about the IRA needing to wear "sackcloth and ashes" and needing to express sorrow. But he said much more. He said he would be "highly honoured" to be First Minister.

"I would like to think that we would have a quiet province, I'd like to think that people said: 'The man of war was a man of peace', but, of course, we have to wait and see… I think we have before us the way it can be done and this really rests on the decommissioning and also the (testing) period afterwards; proving to people that the criminal activities of the IRA and everything connected with terrorism has been put away, and I think if we get there, then we are there, and seeing is believing."

Paisley had made similar comments outside police headquarters in Belfast, indicating that while it would stick in his craw, in the right circumstances he would do the deal, and his deputy, Peter Robinson, believes republicans panicked when they heard these words.

ROBINSON: I think it was then, for the first time that the Republican movement gasped, having up until then always thought that he (Paisley) is going to blink first. You know, there's no way Paisley's going to go (for a deal), and it's simply a case of us keeping focused, keep on through and he'll run away before the end of the process. And, suddenly, they realised that all of what they talked about, they might actually have to do and Paisley was up for it, and I think there was a desperate search around for an exit at this stage… I'm not convinced it's because they didn't want to do a deal, as they didn't feel that they could do a deal at that stage. They hadn't prepared their organisation for the steps that had to be taken… So, I think at that stage they recognised that Ian Paisley was for real, that he was going to go into it, and, in looking for an excuse, they jumped upon a speech that he made in Ballymena – a speech which I think should have been perhaps looked at in more theological terms than political terms. Ian very often speaks in his theological language and what he effectively was saying is we need people who have made a real life change. It isn't simply a case of continuing to be a paramilitary but taking on the role of a politician. You do need to give it up. You do need to change your life, and in his theological terms, sackcloth and ashes and so forth, was very much that, you know, born again feeling.

Paisley wanted a deal, wanted to be the unionist leader who delivered the end of the IRA, but, as far as republicans were concerned, his terms were unacceptable. It would not be easy for him to make "peace" with his republican enemy. That was accepted. But, equally, it would not be easy for republicans to do business with him. They remembered the "Third Force", "Ulster Resistance", "Smash Sinn Féin", his role at Drumcree and, now, there was the "sackcloth and ashes" and all of the inference in that – theologically speaking or not – of an IRA surrender. I am not sure that that penny ever dropped with the DUP. I am not sure that they realised how difficult this was going to be for republicans, and I am not sure they really cared. They were still seeing the bombs and bullets of the IRA. We were also in a situation in which senior figures in the DUP were assessing the prospects for a deal on the basis of the governments' proposals. And it was only very late into this negotiation that the party began to realise that things that were glittering in the British-Irish paper were not gold.

Days after the Ballymena speech, Paisley junior told me that people inside his party now realised that things that they thought were tied down were not – including this issue of visual proof. While he claims he knew this at the time of the "sackcloth and ashes" speech, others in the party still believed the IRA would deliver. It had to, otherwise there would be no deal. Indeed the negotiations continued beyond the words of Ballymena and all of the fall-out of that Paisley moment. On December 4, however, when it met with de Chastelain, the DUP was surprised to learn that the IRA's representative had not yet met the Independent International Commission on Decommissioning. There had been no discussions on photographs, on inventories and on all of the fine detail of decommissioning. But, those of us who have watched the IRA through all of the years and all of the twists and turns of this process were not surprised. The IRA was not going to sign on any dotted line until it was sure of the outcome of the overall negotiations. No one was disputing the scale of what the IRA was preparing itself to do. No one was questioning that the decommissioning process would be completed within the timeframe of a few short weeks. Everyone now accepted that there would be new church witnesses, and, in his own words, P O'Neill was expected to announce an end to all IRA activities. The only major doubt was on this issue of proof. Inside the negotiations there had been much talking about photographs and many words had been written on this subject. But outside the negotiations, in all of the talking I did with republicans, not once did I hear that pictures were possible.

Hours after the DUP meeting with de Chastelain, I spoke to Peter Robinson on the two issues of witnesses and photographs.

"We need absolute certainty that there will be no restrictions on what the witnesses will be able to see," he told me. "They can't be gagged when they come back and, equally, there's no point having photos if nobody is going to see them. We need certainty. We are not going to make assumptions."

In my reporting that evening I said this issue of photographic proof was still a potential "deal-breaker". I wrote: "The DUP and republicans are very close to a deal, but it could all still trip up – not over the extent of IRA decommissioning but on the issue of visible proof." There would not be any of the kind that Paisley wanted, but there would be the "talking eyes".

The following day – Sunday, December 5 – I spoke to two senior republicans. One told me that his personal view was that photographs were always "a non-starter". He said he could not see Adams and McGuinness – even if they wanted to – "being able to persuade the IRA to humiliate itself for Ian Paisley". And, on the extent of what the IRA was prepared to do, he said: "Presumably if all of that is done, in anybody's book what will they conclude? That (it) was definitive, huge, (and) conclusive. They've (the DUP) had their chance and I think they are about to blow it."

On photographs, he told me to "stick with where you are". In other words there was no change in the republican position. In a later conversation he said: "The internal consequences for the republican struggle would be greater than the gain. It couldn't be sustained."

This source had guided me through another crucial phase of the peace process in late 1999-early 2000.

The IRA had appointed a representative to talk to de Chastelain and a power-sharing Executive had been formed, but Trimble made it clear that the life of that government depended on actual decommissioning. The government, many unionists and others believed the IRA would deliver. My source told me they were wrong. They were. He was right and, in February 2000, the then Secretary of State Peter Mandelson had to suspend devolution. My source would also be right this time. There would be no photographs, not now, and not in September 2005, when the IRA eventually moved to complete the decommissioning process.

The second republican I spoke to on December 5 was not involved in the detail of the negotiations, but I knew he would have a sense of the mood inside Sinn Féin, inside the IRA and across the movement. He said there was nobody "dissuading anybody about the media speculation of the enormity of what's on offer (from the IRA)."

"The movement (is) at the point where people know this could be the endgame for them," he said. The one issue that is causing "great consternation", he told me, "is the photographs". It is "a step too far" and something that people "can't live with".

"If Paisley can't do it (the deal), let him fucking say it and we'll see what can be done."

Peter Robinson had never doubted the extent of what the IRA was prepared to do. His concern was always about the "how", and, on the "how", he had to go on the assessments of the governments. He was hearing what they were saying about photographs and he was reading it in their proposals. The pictures were always there, but they were never there. As this negotiation broke down a senior official told me that there had been an assumption that photos would be OK: "Whether there was an assurance is another thing."

On that Sunday, December 5, three days before this negotiation ended, Adams said during an interview on RTE: "Say we get to the point where we have a comprehensive agreement, and say we get the IRA to confirm that it is prepared to put weapons beyond use, and is prepared to go into entirely new mode, and we're all satisfied we are going to see an end to physical force republicanism, is it going to be thrown away because Ian Paisley doesn't get the process of humiliation that he wants?"

Here Adams outlined all of the things that were possible, and pointed to the one thing that wasn't. Another republican put it much more bluntly: "What the fuck else does anyone want? The only other thing they could want is a process of humiliation (and) we aren't going to get people over the line on that."

What the DUP wanted was a deal with the proof of pictures, and a deal in which the former Presbyterian Moderator David McGaughey would be the "talking eyes" of decommissioning. That deal was not on offer – not now and not later. An approach had already been made to someone else – to the Rev Harold Good, who would be the Protestant church witness when the IRA eventually moved some nine months later to put its arms beyond use. The republican position on the proposed comprehensive agreement emerged publicly on December 6, 2004 after a day of private discussions inside the movement. A senior intelligence source told me that "a number of Provos went off peoples' radar", and my source believes this was the day when the IRA had its last word on the limits it was prepared to go to in any deal with Paisley and the governments.

That evening Richard McAuley called me with a number of briefing lines.

SINN FÉIN BRIEFING, DECEMBER 6, 2004: "Senior Sinn Féin leaders are meeting in Belfast this evening. The Sinn Féin President told the meeting that he believes that Sinn Féin can say 'Yes' to the political package as now presented. It is understood that Mr Adams said that he believed that the party's discussions with the two governments have successfully defended the fundamentals of the Good Friday Agreement, resolved issues of concern and succeeded in strengthening key provisions. The meeting did not discuss the issue of IRA weapons. Gerry Adams made it clear that resolving the weapons issue is a matter for the IICD and the armed groups. Sinn Féin believes that it can be resolved to the satisfaction of all reasonable people."

In a nutshell Adams was endorsing the politics and the policing arrangements in the proposed comprehensive agreement, but he wasn't saying "yes" to the photographs of decommissioning.

PETER ROBINSON: It was clear that he wasn't accepting an essential element of the overall proposal. Again it fitted into my general view that they were starting to run for the exits, because they couldn't carry on the arms issue, and they, of course, were dragging up Ian Paisley's remarks (on "sackcloth and ashes") having for a long period of time and in detail continued

All eyes on the IRA – Adams speaks and Oglaigh na hEireann responds.

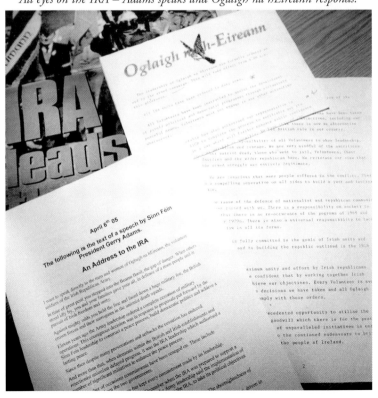

Lord of the Political Ring – After the Belfast Agreement, Ian Paisley is now the undisputed leader of unionism.

*Mistaken Identity – Gerry "garcon" Kelly was consulted
on the Leeds Castle cuisine (see page 73).*

*Story of the Century – Martin McGuinness's description
of a DUP-Sinn Féin government.*

Prod Vision – Can David Ervine and Jackie McDonald help re-invent and re-deliver the loyalism of 1994?

"Doc's" Deputy – Peter Robinson dismisses talk of divisons in the DUP during the '04 negotiations. It seems they were all singing from the same hymn sheet.

April Appeal – Mitchel McLaughlin and the Sinn Féin President pictured just minutes before Adams' April address to the IRA.

Summer Words – Séanna Walsh reads the orders ending the IRA's armed campaign (Photograph IRA DVD).

Talking Eyes – Rev Harold Good, a witness to the IRA's decommissioning.

*Infighting and "Intalking" – Away from the feuding,
the UVF debates its future.*

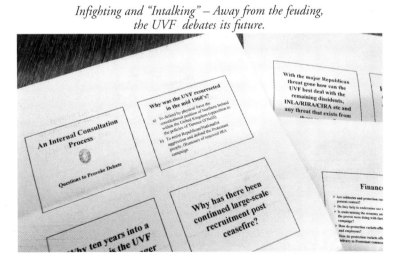

The Kelly Case – Sinn Féin's Gerry Kelly, a key figure in the behind-the-scenes moves leading to the release of the Shankill bomber Sean Kelly.

The Guns General – The author Brian Rowan pictured with General John de Chastelain (Photograph by Aaro Suonio).

negotiations knowing that those remarks had taken place and having already absorbed them.

In London, the DUP was waiting for a number of written commitments from the government on a financial package to accompany the deal, on confidence-building measures, on the future of the Royal Irish Regiment and on the decommissioning photographs and witnesses.

Two of the written responses never came, including what the party had been waiting for on the arms issue.

The following morning Paisley junior called me while he was in the company of his father, who was listening to our conversation. He asked me again how "hard" it would be for republicans to deliver on the issue of photographs. I told him "hard" was an understatement. I had outlined this position many times on radio and television and I would do so again on David Dunseith's *Talkback* programme at noon. I told Dunseith that the IRA had not agreed to the principle of photographic proof and therefore had not agreed to the publication of photographs. And I said that information was "current" and had been gathered "in recent hours" from a number of sources. This possible "deal of all deals" was dying before our eyes – and when its full detail emerged the SDLP would accuse Sinn Féin of giving away key elements of the Good Friday Agreement.

ALEX ATTWOOD: Despite all that negotiation there wasn't any commitments to any further North-South bodies in the comprehensive agreement... Secondly, central to the Good Friday Agreement and to the Assembly was a shared leadership of government in the First and Deputy First Minister – (a) to reassure people that nobody was going to abuse the other side, and (b) in order to send out a big signal to Northern society about a shared society. What did Sinn Féin agree with the DUP? A process to lead to the unpicking of that office...

We negotiated into the Good Friday Agreement that nationalists in government had their own power, and what did Sinn Féin do in the negotiations with the DUP – they shackled the power of ministers and therefore made nationalist ministers accountable and subject to a bigger unionist majority on the Executive.

MARTIN McGUINNESS: We had effectively, and this is where the SDLP didn't see the big picture, at least behind the scenes brought the DUP to a position where they would go out and say one thing about where they stood on the Good Friday Agreement but to all intents and purposes they had accepted the Good Friday Agreement as a template for forward progress, (but) Paisley was still majoring on the issue of photographs.

The DUP like the SDLP believes that significant changes to the Agreement had been secured, but that was only part of their terms for a deal. Blair and Ahern came to Belfast on December 8, 2004 to point to all of the progress that had been made in this latest and long negotiation, and behind the scenes efforts would continue to try to secure the IRA's offer on decommissioning and the ending of activities. These were talks between the British Government and Adams and McGuinness. But then there would be a shock to the political process. There was a bank robbery and it had the circumstantial fingerprints of the IRA all over it.

CHAPTER THREE

THE BANK JOB

"The IRA has been accused of involvement in the recent Northern Bank robbery. We were not involved." P O'Neill, January 2005, speaking for the IRA leadership.

"Quite frankly, my position is that the people who have denied it on behalf of the Provisional IRA have got some brass neck." John Grieve, Independent Monitoring Commission, speaking February 2005.

"Their denials are just as meaningful as Adams' denial: (claiming) he never was in the IRA. It's as simple as that." Senior intelligence officer, speaking October 2005.

"That bank robbery took place in December (2004). They've yet to produce one single coin or note from that robbery which would prove that the IRA were responsible for it." Martin McGuinness, speaking in October 2005.

DECEMBER 21, 2004. The breaking news that Tuesday morning in the run-up to Christmas was the story of a robbery in which a substantial amount of money had been stolen from a Northern Bank. At this early stage, there was little detail and nothing in the bulletin that would have made one's ears listen up – not yet anyway. But, by lunchtime, the scale of what had happened was becoming much clearer. Millions of pounds had been stolen from the Bank's Belfast headquarters in the city centre, and two of its employees and their families had been held hostage during the raid. Hours earlier, the Northern Ireland chief constable Sir Hugh Orde had been wakened out of his sleep. It was one of those "bad news" early morning calls from his assistant chief constable Sam Kinkaid to alert him to a serious incident. What was being talked about in these early hours would become the biggest bank robbery in UK history, and, just weeks after the collapse of that long political negotiation, the IRA's name would soon be attached to the raid. An intelligence assessment provided for this book suggests "at least four" of the organisation's active service units were involved, and that the job was being run by the IRA's most senior "operational managers", including its chief of staff and its Belfast-based director of intelligence. The officer who gave this assessment named both men. He was clearly confirming that this was a job that had come out of the IRA's top drawer – that it had the sanction of the leadership.

"There was an awful lot of activity in the Provisional movement during the month of December, and a lot of it was tied up with the whole business of the talks and there was a presumed act of decommissioning would have followed," a senior intelligence officer told me.

"So, clearly there was a lot of activity running and the sorts of people sometimes involved in that activity were the sort of people who would be organising such a major operation (the bank job)."

I do not intend here to get into the nuts and bolts of this robbery. All I want to do is set it in the context of a negotiation that had just broken down, and then the fall-out in the political process when an IRA label was attached to the £26.5 million raid. Two bank staff whose families were being held captive were forced to hand over the money, and the van used by the gang visited the bank twice.

Those long political negotiations that had spanned the autumn of 2004 were barely cold. There had been little or no time to mourn the fact that a deal had not been done. And, now, here we were looking at something very different – at an IRA job at the level of what has come to be described as the "spectacular". In that moment, it seemed that the business of progress had been buried, but, within months, we had that Adams speech leading to the IRA ending its armed campaign and then the decommissioning. None of that could be seen on that day of the robbery and as the story of the stolen millions emerged.

The senior intelligence officer said: "What you had was, you'd two houses taken over (at Loughinisland in County Down and at Poleglass on the outskirts of west Belfast), and a series of movements of vehicles. Once you start looking at the house takeovers and how the house takeovers were managed and what they did in them, what happened in the movements of the vehicles and how that was organised and what we knew about that; we then started looking back at previous incidents the year before, which we knew the Provos had done, and the way they managed it and the way they did it. That in itself, even if there hadn't been a single source of intelligence coming in from technical or human sources, you would have been putting it to the Provos the way it was managed… It wasn't just from the intelligence. It was from the assessment of the modus operandi they used, the way they went about their business clearly has a small 'p' professionalism that helps them to avoid detection, but it is a distinctive mark of their acts and the way they behave."

On that Tuesday morning, December 21, as the scale of the job began to emerge, the chief constable Sir Hugh Orde knew that the inevitable next question was going to be: Whodunit? Politically the bank job could not have come at a worse time. Very clearly there had been an overlap – the planning for the raid was going on at the same as those long negotiations which had just failed to produce a deal. And, at the time of the robbery, the British Government was still involved in private talks with Adams and McGuinness trying to secure the IRA offer to complete decommissioning and to end activities. Soon, republicans would be accused of acting in "bad faith".

"It was a pretty sophisticated job," Orde told me.

ORDE: That became apparent very quickly… the number of sites, scale, movement of vehicles, keeping people hostage. This was big numbers and we were clear, for a number of reasons fairly quickly, that this had to be PIRA… This was being seen as a great success within certain republican circles, and what was being forgotten was that there were some real victims in this. People could have died. If people hadn't complied they'd have happily killed them. This is what PIRA do. So, it was a particularly brutal and vicious robbery… This was a crime at the top end of violence. People will not recover from this. It was that brutal… This wasn't some Robin Hood effort. This was people robbing people using maximum violence and fear of death to achieve their advantage.

So, soon after the raid, the whodunit argument had already been narrowed down to the IRA.

The intelligence assessment had "at least four ASU's (active service units)" involved.

The senior intelligence officer said: "It means that, all of a sudden, you're into the operational managers of the organisation… M—— and S—— and other people of that nature. That's the only way you're going to co-ordinate an operation with four ASUs."

It took just days for the thinking of those private intelligence assessments to begin to emerge in some public sense. On Christmas Eve the homes of a number of prominent republicans in north and west Belfast were searched.

There were no arrests. But the nature of this search operation put it into the public mind and put it into the political mind that the police now believed that this was an IRA job. The searches were confirming everyone's suspicions. Eddie Copeland's house was searched in north Belfast and John Trainor's in the west of the city. Just a few months earlier, he had a prominent role in the guard of honour at the funeral of the veteran IRA leader Joe Cahill. Twenty-four hours before the searches, the IRA had issued its first public denial of involvement in the robbery. Adams and McGuinness said they believed them. Hardly anyone else did.

The top policing job in Northern Ireland is very different from the many others in the United Kingdom. Here, assessments given by the Chief Constable can have huge political implications. Orde knew that, and so, he thought for eighteen days and eighteen nights before giving his first public assessment. This was on January 7, 2005 at the offices of the Policing Board – the body tasked with holding the PSNI to account. I knew how things were shaping up and, the day before on *Radio Ulster*, I said the following:

"…there is a growing sense that when he (Orde) puts a label on this robbery that he will point towards the IRA. And if that is confirmed as the policing assessment, then I don't think it will be long before we have the political fall-out."

Orde said it was the IRA, and he didn't offer up any other possibilities – all main lines of inquiry currently undertaken were in that direction.

ORDE: We wanted to do proper appeals and the only question (from journalists and politicians) was: Who did it? Who did it? Who did it? So it was just getting in the way which meant my investigators couldn't do their job properly. So, my decision, my view, was something had to be said, and if you are going to say something like that, there's only one person who can do it, because if you got it wrong you're out, and that would be unfair. So, I did it.

ROWAN: And did you think it was that serious, you get it wrong and you're out?

ORDE: Oh yeah, oh yeah. That is where this job is unique in terms of chief (constable) jobs. (A): No other chief has to deal with that sort of stuff, and (B): It's making damn sure you're doing it for policing reasons, not political reasons, which you really had to think about as well, and (C): If you're going to do it, then you take the hit, you take the hit.

ROWAN: You were clearly satisfied that you got it right.

ORDE: I made damn sure... You have to be as sure as you can be... Can I justify what I said with the knowledge I had at the time I said it? Yes I can... I was convinced... No one actually challenged me that much... This (the IRA) is an organisation which is almost Stalinist in nature ... The notion that a job like that could be carried out without authority is just off beam.

ROWAN: Sanctioned from the top?

ORDE: It had to be, had to be.

Orde's assistant Sam Kinkaid, the "bad news" caller on that early morning line on Tuesday, December 21, had all of the intelligence assessed and all of the strands of the investigation assessed before the Chief Constable spoke publicly.

Orde was not exaggerating. Big policing and political reputations were being put on the line. This was too big a call, in terms of public attribution, to get wrong. What the Chief Constable said was the policing assessment both North and South of the border – an assessment that was accepted by both governments right up to the level of Blair and Ahern. Indeed, the Taoiseach went further and described it as a Provisional IRA job "that would have been known to the political leadership". Republicans knew exactly what he was saying. Sinn Féin's Mitchel McLaughlin described this as "a direct attack on the integrity of Gerry Adams and Martin McGuinness". But Ahern's comments were never withdrawn, and the policing assessment was endorsed by the Independent Monitoring Commission – the ceasefire watchdog. In a report on February 10, it said the IRA leadership had not only sanctioned the Northern Bank raid but a series of other robberies – major robberies that were dwarfed by the scale of this one in which £26.5 million had been stolen:

"We have carefully scrutinised all the material of different kinds that has become available to us since the robbery, which leads us to conclude firmly that it was planned and undertaken by the Provisional IRA... In our view Sinn Féin must bear its share of responsibility for all the incidents. Some of its senior members, who are also senior members of PIRA, were involved in sanctioning the series of robberies."

The Irish Justice Minister Michael McDowell would not name names, but said the Sinn Féin leaders who sat on the Army Council were household names regularly seen on television. The McDowell commentary and what had been said earlier by Ahern meant that in Dublin the political gloves were off. Adams said McDowell and the Taoiseach had to "face up to the import of their remarks, have us arrested, bring us forward into the due process".

About a week before that IMC report, the IRA had taken its December 2004 statement off the table – the statement in which it said it was prepared to go into a "new mode", complete the decommissioning process and have that witnessed by two churchmen. It also said that "the seriousness of the situation" should not be underestimated. This was being interpreted as a threat, and republicans refused to explain what was meant, or to dismiss people's worst fears.

ROWAN: There was a lot of discussion at that time that the ceasefire may have been under threat... Did you think at that time that things had gone to the line, or do you think that was people getting carried away?

ORDE: Well I'm on record ad nauseam as saying, on the best information I have, and it was pretty good, there was no indication of a return to a violent campaign.

ROWAN: It wasn't on?
ORDE: I don't think so.

By mid-February the police believed they had made a major breakthrough in their investigation. In raids in the Republic, many of them in Cork, millions of pounds were found. The Garda Commissioner Noel Conroy confirmed this was an investigation into IRA money laundering and soon, a link would be made to the Northern Bank millions.

"A lot of the Cork money was £20 notes – used £20 notes – from all the Banks here in Northern Ireland," a senior intelligence officer said.

"If you actually discount the Northern Bank robbery, there's not enough £20 notes stolen in Northern Ireland to account for the number that was got in the South… The other thing is that all the £20 notes were still in bundles of £20 notes, and not only in bundles, all the Ulster Bank (notes) were together, all the Bank of Ireland… Now the things that were stolen out of the Northern Bank were actually already made up into those bundles. All they did was re-package them."

The intelligence information that grew out of this investigation in the South was that this was the "Provos' Northern Bank money".

"Once the stuff started coming out of Cork, after Cork, the Provos even stopped denying they did it," the senior intelligence officer said. But, twenty-four hours after the Cork raids there was another twist in this story. Fifty thousand pounds in new Northern Bank notes were found in toilets at a police sports club in south Belfast. There had been a search at the club after an anonymous call to the office of the Police Ombudsman. The caller claimed to be a police officer and said drugs had been hidden at the Newforge Club. No drugs were found. The money was and the PSNI confirmed it was linked to the Belfast bank raid. The questions were obvious: Who put it there and why? It was all too obvious as far as the police were concerned – they believed the IRA had planted the money.

"To me that was the icing on the cake," the senior intelligence officer told me.

"That was so stupid. Only a criminal gang with a political agenda would have put the money in the police social club… What are we saying, that your average bank robbers out there would have sat in some bar one night mulling over: what are we going to do with all of this money? Oh let's go back and run the risk of being caught. Only a criminal gang with a political agenda would have thought of putting that money in there, but even then they were stupid. They phoned the Ombudsman… The guy was reading a script. You could hear the paper turning. It was that put up… Which organised crime gang – non-paramilitary – would be interested? None; only someone that was trying to embarrass the police, particularly in the light of what was happening in Cork, and they knew the game was up."

In an interview the following day – February 20, 2005 – the Chief Constable said what the police were thinking.

ORDE: It's a distraction. It is people trying to take the focus off the key issue, which is the operation run by the Garda and the major crime inquiry we still have ongoing… I am not particularly impressed by it, but I did ask them (the IRA) to give the money back in my first press conference, and they have started to listen.

On Monday, February 21, the Sinn Féin MPs Gerry Adams and Martin McGuinness and the TD Martin Ferris issued a joint statement. It was a response to earlier comments by the Irish Justice Minister, Michael McDowell.

"We want to state categorically that we are not members of the IRA or its Army Council. Our involvement in the peace process is as leaders of Sinn Féin and as elected representatives for West

Belfast, Mid-Ulster and Kerry North respectively. As part of this, in the past we have met with the Army Council to put propositions regarding the peace process... Recently the Irish Government accused Martin McGuinness and Gerry Adams of withholding information and of conspiring to rob the Northern Bank in December. We challenged the government to stand this accusation up and they failed to do so. And then at the weekend Michael McDowell made his unfounded and serious allegation that we – Martin McGuinnes, Martin Ferris and Gerry Adams – are members of the IRA Army Council... If this view is shared by the Gardai then the only way this issue can be confronted is for us to be charged with IRA membership."

This statement did not change the political and policing assessment of where these three men sit in the republican hierarchy. But something else is unchanged.

The denial of IRA involvement is still made, and the question is asked back: Where is the proof? This is an interview with Martin McGuinness recorded for this book in October 2005. While he denies it, the policing and political assessments still say he is one of the IRA's most senior leaders, as well as being Sinn Féin's chief negotiator.

ROWAN: Do you still say that the IRA didn't do the bank job?
McGUINNESS: Absolutely, and we told both the British Government and the Irish Government that that was our view. And I am on the record as saying that whoever did the bank job were no friends of the peace process and were no friends of the Sinn Féin leadership. Obviously that was hugely damaging. Michael McDowell obviously latched onto that. It was Michael McDowell who began the whole debate about (IRA) criminality. That came almost in the immediate aftermath of (Irish Foreign Minister) Dermot Ahern's visit to Hillsborough Castle, whenever he came out to the front of the castle and, in a now fairly famous interview, stated his

belief that at some stage in the future he could envisage the prospect of Sinn Féin in government – in a coalition government – in Dublin. So, I think that sent McDowell into an awful spin.

McDowell probably thought that the prospect of the Progressive Democrats being in government in perpetuity with Fianna Fail was guaranteed. And the rise in the Sinn Féin vote in the South was obviously seen by him as a threat to that prospect.

ROWAN: But you've a problem if that bank job is pinned on the IRA?

McGUINNESS: Absolutely, but I don't believe that that will be the case.

ROWAN: But what about (Noel) Conroy (the Garda Commissioner) saying there's no question now in the South?

McGUINNESS: Well it's one thing saying I believe there's no question; you look at the fact that we are now into the tenth month of this year. That bank robbery took place in December (2004); they've yet to produce one single coin or note from that robbery which would prove that the IRA were responsible for it.

ROWAN: They say the Cork money is the bank money.

McGUINNESS: Well, that's what they say, but the people of Ireland are still waiting on the cast iron, gold-plated guarantee that that is the case, but all that they've got from different interviews is a belief or a stated view that that is the case. Whatever about all of that, and whatever about what was going on in Cork, the fact is that the two governments, the two police forces, have failed to connect the IRA to that robbery. Michael McDowell has now majored on the issue of criminality, something that Paisley didn't do during the course of the autumn (2004) negotiations, and obviously in many ways Michael McDowell has provided for Paisley yet another excuse as to why he shouldn't go into government.

The bank job, and the cast iron belief that the IRA did do it –
something which it seems is believed everywhere except inside the
republican community – is what brought the spotlight back onto
the issue of criminality. And long before the robbery and long
before Michael McDowell's comments, the DUP was focused on
all IRA activities – paramilitary and criminal. That is why the
party was arguing for a "testing period" in the event of any deal
emerging out of those autumn negotiations in 2004 – a testing
period to ensure that all IRA activities had ended. Remember Jim
Allister's October comments that republicans "must also
irreversibly abandon criminality including fund-raising by heist."
The only question that is now asked about the raid is around
whether the IRA would have gone through with it if a deal had
been achieved those couple of weeks earlier. I suppose there are
several possibilities. There are those who believe the job was so
well advanced in its planning that the IRA would not have
abandoned it even if the autumn talks had produced a deal. The
thinking behind this argument is that the organisation would not
have walked away from the millions it knew it could have. Of
course, the IRA would not consider this to be criminality. This
was money to sustain its organisation.

In October 2005, a senior intelligence officer gave me this
assessment of the IRA's financial activities. This is three months
after the July 28 statement ordering an end to its armed
campaign.

"All the financial stuff and the financial organisation still exists
intact, absolutely no doubt about that.

"The organised crime activities are still going on – the re-
investment, the money laundering, the revenue offences right
through to various offences to do with VAT… It's a very expensive
organisation to run and that continues. Its financial structure has
to be intact. It cannot rely on legal means of gathering finance."

In this October '05 assessment of the IRA's structure, the senior
intelligence officer said he had "seen nothing to indicate" that the

IRA Army Council had stood down, but he stressed that these were early assessments.

"I'm not saying that they are going to continue in the present structure, but I've seen nothing to indicate to me that the current structure is stood down. Now, I do see a lot of chat, and people are saying how do we do this and how do we organise that, and, ultimately, I agree with the Chief Constable, it's not what they are doing, it's what they are not doing and the whole issue is: Is the Provisional movement going to become part of mainstream civic society?" he said.

That assessment that the IRA cannot sustain its organisation through legal finances is, I'm sure, something that the DUP will want to explore with the police and the Independent Monitoring Commission, and its report in January 2006 will be read to see what is said about the financial structures of the IRA. There is another view, of course, of the December 2004 bank job; that it would not have happened had the political deal been done those couple of weeks earlier. There is also the possibility, I suppose, that it was done by the IRA to manage some internal situation. What would have been the thinking and the mood inside that organisation after two failed political negotiations – one in which David Trimble walked away from a deal, and the other in which business was not completed with Paisley? In both situations, the IRA had declared its hand, and one interpretation was that it got nothing in return. So it is possible that the bank job was the IRA leadership's way of demonstrating to its membership what it was still capable of in terms of so-called "spectacular" operations. Was this the IRA saying it would not be humiliated?

Peter Robinson told me in an interview: "A lot of people say, well, you know, you were very fortunate that you hadn't done the deal or you'd have been caught out very badly. The reality is we wouldn't have been caught out at all."

ROBINSON: Our agreement required an end to criminality and the timetable (including a testing period before the DUP would enter government with Sinn Féin) was such that we wouldn't have been caught out by it. But I think it was an object lesson to everybody that, you know, people who were pretending to be negotiating in good faith with the government were actually planning a bank robbery.

ROWAN: Do you think that job would have happened had the deal been done?

ROBINSON: Well I'm down to just guesswork at that stage. I think if it had happened they (republicans) would have known that it would have wrecked the process. That's all I can say... The whole house of cards would have fallen at that stage.

An end to all IRA criminality remains part of the test that the DUP has set for republicans before there can be a power-sharing government with Sinn Féin. And Robinson is of the view that while the IRA continues to hold the money from the Northern Bank robbery, then it continues to be involved in crime.

The Bank reduced the damage of the robbery by re-calling its notes and changing their design. And a significant chunk of the money was found in those raids in the Republic – as part of that investigation into IRA money laundering. But the bank job hasn't been forgotten and hasn't been erased by the IRA's July 2005 statement and its subsequent decommissioning. Like the photographs which proved to be an impossible demand to meet in the 2004 negotiations, could we now be looking at another insurmountable obstacle – the suggestion from Peter Robinson that the bank money be given up and given back? Just weeks after the Northern Bank robbery in December 2004, the IRA was back in the news again. There was a murder in Belfast city centre, and six women were about to emerge in a very public campaign for justice. The IRA was still in the political dock.

FOOTNOTE

At the start of November 2005, detectives investigating the robbery carried out searches and made several arrests. A number of men have since appeared in court, one of them charged directly with the robbery and kidnapping a bank official and his wife. In a prepared statement the man denied the charges, and also denied being a member of the Provisional IRA.

CHAPTER FOUR

MURDER IN THE MARKETS

"The IRA representatives detailed the outcome of the internal disciplinary proceedings thus far and stated in clear terms that the IRA was prepared to shoot the people directly involved in the killing of Robert McCartney." IRA leadership statement, March 8, 2005.

"What surprised me about the whole of that event was how badly they got it wrong. They're normally good at media management. I think they got it disastrously wrong, and I was staggered when I heard they said they were going to shoot people." Chief Constable Sir Hugh Orde, speaking in October 2005.

"One thing is absolutely true. Robert McCartney was murdered. I believe he was murdered by people who would claim to be republicans. I think they are an absolute disgrace." Martin McGuinness speaking in October 2005.

In the small sitting room in a house in west Belfast, the IRA man spoke to us in a way that could only be described as matter-of-fact. It was half-past three on Tuesday afternoon, March 8 2005, and, the day before, representatives of the IRA leadership had held a second meeting with Robert McCartney's sisters and his partner Bridgeen Hagans in the Short Strand in east Belfast. They had already been told what I was about to read in a detailed five-page statement that had just been handed to me by P O'Neill. On the third of those pages, there was a line that jumped out. It was a line that was meant to do just that – a sentence in which the IRA said it was "prepared to shoot the people directly involved in the killing of Robert McCartney". I asked for an explanation of "shoot", but there was no elaboration, and the possibility that the IRA meant "execute" was left to linger. My journalist colleague Eamonn Mallie was also in the room. We asked again and again for "shoot" to be explained, but the statement was left to speak for itself, and we were left to wonder, did the IRA mean punish or kill? An organisation supposedly under huge pressure because of the Northern Bank robbery was now publicly threatening to use its guns. And, if that pressure existed, it could not be found in this statement and it could not be seen in the man who sat beside me.

This statement from the IRA was to say publicly what the McCartney family had been told privately. It was the IRA outlining the outcome of its "internal disciplinary proceedings" – the decisions of courts martial inside its organisation. By March 8, we already knew that the IRA had "dismissed" three of its men, two of whom were "high-ranking volunteers". One of them – a man from the Short Strand in east Belfast where Robert McCartney had lived – held one of the most senior positions in the organisation's leadership. There had been an earlier statement from the IRA given to RTE News on February 25:

"The investigation established that the IRA was not involved in this incident. We made this clear publicly in a statement issued on February 16. However some republicans were involved… No materials under the control of or belonging to the IRA were produced or used at any time during this savage attack."

That "savage attack" happened in a narrow little street close to Magennis's Bar in the Markets area of Belfast. There had been a fight inside the pub, which then spilled outside. Robert McCartney and a friend, Brendan Devine, were each stabbed. It happened on Sunday night, January 30 2005, and Robert McCartney died the following day. So, just weeks after the bank robbery, the IRA's name was being attached to this murder in the Markets.

No one was suggesting that the IRA leadership had ordered or authorised this killing, but IRA members were involved both in the murder and in the forensic clean-up of the scene. Republicans do not dispute this. It was these people that the McCartney family wanted handed over to the police and into the justice system. Here again, I am not going to dwell on the fine detail of this murder and what has happened since. What I want to do is set this killing in the context of what was happening – or not happening – politically, and the questions it posed for the IRA organisation. The "sitting room" statement of March 8 was the IRA leadership again putting its position on-the-record – and doing so in some considerable detail.

IRA STATEMENT: Representatives of Oglaigh na hEireann met with Bridgeen Hagans, the partner of Robert McCartney, and with his sisters before our statement of 25 February was issued.

The meeting lasted five and a half hours. During this time the IRA representatives gave the McCartney family a detailed account of our investigation.

Our investigation found that after the initial melee in Magennis's Bar a crowd spilled out onto the street and Robert McCartney, Brendan Devine and two other men were pursued into Market Street.

- Four men were involved in the attacks in Market Street on the evening of 30 January. A fifth person was at the scene. He took no part in the attacks and was responsible for moving to safety one of the two people accompanying Robert McCartney and Brendan Devine.
- One man was responsible for providing the knife that was used in the stabbing of Robert McCartney and Brendan Devine in Market Street. He got the knife from the kitchen of Magennis's Bar.

- Another man stabbed Robert McCartney and Brendan Devine.

   (The statement did not specify this, but the man who allegedly provided the knife, and the man who allegedly used it, are two of the three men expelled by the IRA after courts martial.)
- A third man kicked and beat Robert McCartney after he had been stabbed in Market Street.
- A fourth man hit a friend of Robert McCartney and Brendan Devine across the face with a steel bar in Market Street.
- The man who provided the knife also retrieved it from the scene and destroyed it.

   (The statement did not give this information, but it is understood the knife was ground down into dust).

The same man also took the CCTV tape from the bar, after threatening a member of staff, and later destroyed it. He also burned clothes after the attack.

Reports in the media have alleged that up to twelve IRA volunteers were involved in the events in Market Street. Our investigation found that this is not so. Of the four people directly involved in the attacks in Market Street, two were IRA volunteers. The other two were not. The IRA knows the identity of all these men.

The build-up to the attack and stabbings was also outlined to the family and subsequently set out publicly in the IRA's statement of 25 February.

The IRA representatives detailed the outcome of the internal disciplinary proceedings thus far and stated in clear terms that the IRA was prepared to shoot the people directly involved in the killing of Robert McCartney.

The McCartney family raised their concerns with the IRA representatives.

These included:

Firstly, the family made it clear that they did not want physical action taken against those involved. They stated that they wanted those individuals to give a full account of their actions in court.

Secondly, they raised concerns about the intimidation of witnesses.

The IRA's position on this was set out in unambiguous and categoric terms on February 15 and February 25.

Before and after this meeting with the family the IRA gave direct assurances on their safety to three named individuals who the family believe were the targets of intimidation. Since we met the family, at that time, the good offices of an independent third party have been employed to reinforce these assurances with two of the three men. To this point the third party has not been able to contact the other man.

We have urged any witnesses who can assist in any way to come forward. That remains our position. The only interest the IRA has in this case is to see truth and justice achieved.

Since we issued our statement on February 25 there has been much political and media comment on what we had to say. Predictably our opponents and enemies who have their own agendas have used this brutal killing to attack republicans and to advance their own narrow political interests. The public will make their own judgement on this.

We sought and held a second meeting with the McCartney family in the presence of an independent observer.

In the course of this we reiterated our position in respect of witnesses, including our view that all witnesses should come forward. We also revisited details of the incident.

We disclosed the following to the family:

The conclusions of the IRA's investigations are based on voluntary admissions by those involved.

The names of those involved in the attacks and stabbings of Robert McCartney, Brendan Devine and the assault on another man in Market Street were given to the family.

This included the names of the two men responsible for providing the knife, using the knife, destroying the knife, destroying the CCTV tape and burning clothes.

In addition we informed the family that:

We have ordered anyone who was present on the night to go forward and to give a full and honest account of their actions. That includes those who have already been subject to the IRA's internal disciplinary proceedings.

We are continuing to press all of those involved in the events around the killing of Robert McCartney to come forward. The IRA is setting out all of the above at length because it is important that those issues of truth and justice are successfully resolved.

We are doing our best to work with the family and to respect their wishes.

The following day, I interviewed Catherine McCartney at the home of her sister Paula in the Short Strand – a home she has since had to leave. I asked Catherine if she had been shocked by what the IRA had told her the organisation was prepared to do – to shoot the killers of her brother.

"We are not naïve. The IRA as an organisation is a guerrilla organisation and they have dealt with these sorts of things before and that's the way they have dealt with it in the past. But for us the bottom line is, and it would have been if it had been in the middle of the Troubles, we still would have wanted these people in court, because this was a murder that was not carried out for any reason whatsoever, and the IRA told us at that meeting; we asked them if they had been speaking to these people, could these people even give a reason why they murdered Robert that night, and the IRA representatives were very open with us and they said there was no reason.

ROWAN: Do you think the family saying "No" saved the life of the killer of your brother?

CATHERINE McCARTNEY: Well, when you go back to the start when this happened, and I don't want to go into the maybe they would have, maybe they wouldn't have; the IRA may have taken action against them, but this family has had to campaign endlessly to get anybody to take responsibility for this, and then it was two weeks – maybe two and a half weeks – later that responsibility did start to get taken by the organisation… People should not be asking us: What do you want the IRA to do, what do you want Sinn Féin to do? They are organisations like any other organisations; they go and they should be discussing the strategy of how we get from A to B… I do not believe that the IRA, who remember are nearly a hundred years old in their history, are probably one of the most notorious guerrilla warfare machines in the world, and have been known for that, and they cannot resolve this issue.

The Short Strand is a small Catholic island surrounded by a loyalist sea. It is an area that the IRA defended at the very start of the Troubles – a place where Sinn Féin won its first political seat in 2001. Joe O'Donnell was elected as a councillor in the Pottinger Ward and, at the time of the McCartney murder, was deputy mayor of Belfast. Sinn Féin would lose its seat in the local elections of 2005 – just one of the impacts of this killing. It was a murder that split the republican community in this area – that put the "external" IRA leadership into conflict with the "internal" IRA leadership in the Short Strand. Some held the view that one of the three men expelled by the republican organisation had been "hung out to dry".

"The community was torn," one source told me.

"It (the killing) caused huge disquiet among the republican community. They were shocked to discover that IRA volunteers would be involved in such an incident, and they were deeply concerned that IRA volunteers would be involved in a cover up."

In the May 2005 council elections, the Sinn Féin seat was lost for a number of reasons – that "lifelong supporters" of the party and the IRA "couldn't get over the killing", and that others wouldn't vote because they didn't like how the "outside" leadership had handled things – and in particular its treatment of a local IRA leader – a man who had held one of the most senior positions in the organisation's command structure, and a republican of some considerable standing still in the Short Strand.

The IRA in its "sitting room" statement of March 8 said it was doing its best to respect the family's wishes. But Robert McCartney's partner Bridgeen Hagans and one of his sisters, Paula, who had homes in the Short Strand, say they were eventually forced to leave. They were subjected to intimidation. Again, no one is suggesting that this was authorised by the IRA leadership, but it happened, and a family campaigning and demanding justice for a murdered loved one, was seen to suffer more. We know that the IRA expelled those it alleged were directly involved in the murder – the man who it claimed had stabbed both Robert McCartney and Brendan Devine, and the man who it claimed had supplied and then destroyed the knife. Sinn Féin suspended "without prejudice" a number of its members. Some were later re-instated and others resigned. Gerry Adams visited the family on a number of occasions and invited them to be present and to hear his address to the Sinn Féin Ard Fheis – the party's annual conference. The IRA – through leadership representatives – also visited the family and said its only interest was to see truth and justice achieved. This was the republican leadership publicly placing itself on the side of the family – the five McCartney sisters, Gemma, Paula, Catherine, Donna and Claire and Robert's partner Bridgeen Hagans. In a statement at Easter, the IRA said the killing was "wrong, it was murder, it was a crime".

IRA STATEMENT: But it was not carried out by the IRA, nor was it carried out on behalf of the IRA. The IRA moved quickly to deal with those involved. We have tried to assist in whatever way we can. Unfortunately, it would appear that no matter what we do it will not be enough for some.

A week earlier, President Bush and some of the most senior political figures in the United States had opened their doors to the McCartney family. So too have Tony Blair and Bertie Ahern, as well as many other senior and significant politicians. This was the stuff of high politics, but, on the ground under the surface of this case, the family was still being subjected to intimidation. Its search for justice was being obstructed, if not by the IRA as such, then by republicans. This, again, is something that is not disputed by the Sinn Féin leadership.

"Well, the McCartney case was absolutely horrific," Martin McGuinness said in October 2005.

McGUINNESS: It was terrible, not just because of the incident and the way the man was murdered, but the way that impacted on the overall political situation was very damaging indeed. There was never at any stage any suggestion that the leadership of the IRA had authorised the killing of Robert McCartney. Everybody accepts that the killing of Robert McCartney happened because of a row in a bar – alcohol was involved. Some terrible rubbish has been put out about what actually happened. The one that you hear all the time in America: How could seventy people have been in a toilet whenever Robert McCartney was killed in the bar? And, when people are told that Robert McCartney wasn't killed in the bar, he was killed in a side street by people who followed him out into the street, and that seventy people in the bar didn't see who killed Robert McCartney, people then say: 'Well that's not the story we were hearing.' So, there's all sorts of rubbish talked about the McCartney case. But one thing is absolutely true – Robert McCartney was murdered. I believe he was murdered by people who would claim to be republicans. I think they are an absolute disgrace, and I passionately hope that whoever murdered Robert McCartney, if they are guilty (that they) are found guilty of that and sent to prison. Now, what more can I do about that? People will then say, but there's a conspiracy among these people in the Short Strand to prevent the truth coming out. I believe there is a conspiracy among those people to prevent the truth coming out. How do I bring the truth out?

ROWAN: Do you think the IRA have done all they can in terms of that case?

McGUINNESS: Oh, absolutely.

ROWAN: In terms of their help for the family?

McGUINNESS: No doubt whatsoever, but I also understand where the family are coming from, because the family can see things, like republicans who are avowedly for the peace process who are trying to mediate in a situation, going over and talking to different people in what is a very tragic situation for the people of Short Strand. The people of Short Strand are good, decent people, but they have been torn apart by this particular murder, but they (the McCartney family) see mediation going on and they misinterpret that as some sort of loyalty by the IRA for the people (involved in the killing) and, in my opinion, under no circumstances is that what's going on. Many others within the leadership of Sinn Féin would share my concern if we thought for one minute that people were giving succour to those who murdered Robert McCartney. That's not on the agenda.

Intimidation of the family was clearly on the agenda of some others, and the IRA was unable to stop it. No one is suggesting that this murder was authorised by the leadership of that organisation, no one is suggesting that the intimidation was authorised by the leadership of that organisation, but the know-how learned within the IRA was put to use by those involved. This is the conspiracy that Martin McGuinness referred to, and it was something that became immediately apparent as the police investigation developed.

SIR HUGH ORDE: It shows the sort of people we are still dealing with. And the question (is): Are they out of control in their own organisation? How much grip has PIRA got on these players, if they feel they can do that... and then use the machine to protect them... The machine was as efficient as the machine has always been in terms of operating intimidation, cleaning up, forensic awareness (and) the number of people in that pub who saw nothing. All that plays. The one thing that they really underestimated was the family. They badly underestimated the family – articulate, determined (and) cohesive and it grabbed the international mind.

ROWAN: When you say the machine, you don't for one minute believe that the IRA on that night authorised that killing?

ORDE: No I don't. There's no evidence to suggest that. I think it is a good indicator of the sort of things we might find ourselves dealing with. It's around people who think they are in powerful positions because they can rule by intimidation, fear and terror, and they thought they were doing it on the back of an organisation. The problem they have now is, the organisation is saying: We ain't here anymore. So, the big step now is what do Sinn Féin do about it. How do the politics manage that process? And, at some stage, if they join the Policing Board, that's a fairly clear statement of intent that these people (involved in such crimes) are going to be given up.

Orde told me he was "staggered" when he heard the IRA say it was prepared to shoot those involved, and he watched an organisation normally so good at media management, get this one "disastrously wrong". Sinn Féin's rival for the nationalist vote, the SDLP, also believes that republicans underestimated the family.

"How anybody thought that justice could be served by committing a murder after a murder is just simply outrageous," said SDLP policing spokesman Alex Attwood.

"It was warped logic and it raised fundamental questions about what the IRA's wider intentions were."

Attwood believes the IRA's hand was forced by the family – by the five sisters and by Robert McCartney's partner.

"The IRA rely upon people not standing against them, that they will remain quiet. But when they stand up and shout loud, people are very powerful."

CATHERINE McCARTNEY: We can never give up. It's frustrating, it is exhausting and you just don't have a life.

Catherine was speaking to me just weeks after her brother's murder.

CATHERINE McCARTNEY: But we will never be able to close this. If we ever do feel deflated, the image we have in our minds is Robert lying in Market Street stabbed while another man continued to kick him and then others helped in a cover-up.

As I write, two men are facing charges in connection with the murder of Robert McCartney and the stabbing of Brendan Devine. Those attacks and the bank job were the backdrop to the speech by Gerry Adams in April 2005, when he asked the IRA to leave the stage. That organisation responded by ending its armed campaign and moving to complete the decommissioning process. We know that such moves were being considered long before the robbery and the McCartney killing. They were on offer during the negotiations in the autumn of 2004, and they were being thought about inside republicanism even before then. But some hold the view that the stance taken by "democratic nationalism" right across Ireland after these incidents was so solid that it prompted the IRA to move quickly and unilaterally. Part of that move was the decision of the organisation to put it arms beyond use.

CHAPTER FIVE

NO GUNS, NOW GOVERNMENT?

"We believe that the arms decommissioned represent the totality of the IRA's arsenal." General John de Chastelain, September 26, 2005.

"Beyond any shadow of doubt, the arms of the IRA have now been decommissioned." Rev Harold Good, September 26, 2005.

"The IRA leadership can now confirm that the process of putting our arms beyond use has been completed." P O'Neill, September 26, 2005.

"Instead of openness there was the cunning tactics of a cover-up." Ian Paisley, September 26, 2005.

The journey to the meeting place followed a familiar pattern – a number of vehicle changes and then into a car with blacked out windows. It was September 2005, and the two military men were about to meet again, the decommissioning general John de Chastelain and the senior IRA leader Brian Keenan. They had known each other a long time, as long as the IRA's involvement in the decommissioning process which stretches back to a first meeting in December 1999. The general has never disclosed Keenan's identity, nor has anyone involved in the September acts of decommissioning. John de Chastelain only ever talks about

"O'Neill", but he did tell me that his commission had always "dealt with the same representative". It has been an on-off engagement, a talking, not talking kind of existence, but, through all of the fall-outs of the political process, their working relationship survived, and here they where – de Chastelain and Keenan – on a day that few had ever thought possible. The general defined the relationship as "purely professional and purely focused on the issue of decommissioning", and he said a trust had developed "that each would do what they said they would do". The men of decommissioning were dealing with the rawest issue of all – the business of the IRA's guns.

There were others at the meeting place – the general's colleagues in the IICD, Brigadier Tauno Nieminen and Andrew Sens plus two churchmen, the Rev Harold Good and Father Alex Reid – the new watching and witnessing eyes in this latest and must crucial phase of decommissioning. Their introduction at a secret venue somewhere, but who knows where, on the island of Ireland, was when de Chastelain first learned who would accompany him on this latest mission to put the IRA's arms beyond use. He had not known up to this point. The preparatory work for this day had begun some weeks earlier. Sens and de Chastelain met the IRA "shortly" before its July 28 announcement when it ordered an end to its armed campaign. The decommissioning men were given an indication that the IRA was moving to "endgame" and de Chastelain and his colleague discussed with that organisation's representative when they were likely to be needed again.

"We agreed we would come back on call," de Chastelain told me, "or come back ourselves at the beginning of September."

Implicit in the meeting was that the IRA had work to do before then – the gathering-up of its weapons and explosives. What was now intended was not another act of decommissioning but the completion of the process, whatever completion can mean in business of this kind.

This was the added significance, that this was the end point in a journey beyond ceasefires and beyond the language of not a bullet, not an ounce – and look who was there. Keenan had told a republican audience back in 1996, that the only decommissioning the IRA was interested in was the British State out of Ireland. In the public eye he has always been one of the IRA's hard men – one of its "hawks" – but without him, without his support and the support of other senior IRA figures, Adams and McGuinness could not have moved the process to this point. It was the former Northern Ireland Chief Constable Sir Ronnie Flanagan who once told me that if you could feel Keenan's pulse, then you had the pulse of the IRA. The Belfast republican would always have been one of the targets of the watching eyes and listening ears of the intelligence services. He was that significant – that important. One intelligence source described Keenan as "a big supporter of the bearded one (meaning Adams)".

"He pulled a lot of people over (to his side) at the Convention, him and Brian Gillen (another Belfast republican). They swung it."

He was talking about the IRA General Army Convention of 1997, which led to the emergence of the dissident "Real" IRA – the organisation responsible for the Omagh bomb in 1998. But the vast bulk of the IRA organisation remained with Adams and McGuinness. They won that Convention debate, and my intelligence source was suggesting that Keenan was a key factor in that outcome. There was no suggestion in what he was saying that Keenan had gone "soft", so to speak. It was the fact that he had been such a driving force within the IRA that gave him the influence he now had as that organisation moved in a different direction. Keenan moved with it, moved with Adams and McGuinness, and they took with them the numbers and the people they needed. The dissidents had not been able to present an alternative strategy, and, without Keenan and others like him on their side, had not been able to offer up any viable alternative in terms of a new political and military leadership. They had been outmanoeuvred in that secret Convention of 1997.

A Belfast republican, who has watched Keenan inside the IRA for thirty years and more, said he was someone who was held in the "highest esteem, from the volunteers on the ground to the Army Council".

"The reason for that; he was there at the start," my source told me. "He was on the ground on active service at different stages in the North, in Britain and in other theatres of operation. He led from the front when the war was on and he was pivotal in supporting the peace process. I would go as far as to say that he almost single-handedly brought the IRA with the peace process at crucial stages whenever it could all have gone disastrously wrong… If he had opposed the ceasefire strategy, it would have gone nowhere."

That also means that had he opposed the decommissioning process, it too would have gone nowhere. My source could not confirm that Keenan was the IRA representative in the de Chastelain talks, but what he could confirm was that he was one of the few who would have had the credentials to do that job. In every sense, this was a potential "poison chalice", but he believed Keenan "had the integrity and the strength of character to handle that. He's a heavyweight intellectually and a heavyweight in terms of the Army (the IRA)."

The events of September, this putting beyond use of the IRA's arsenal, did not come cheaply. As soon as the IRA spoke in July, there was an immediate British military response, a move to take down one of the watchtowers in south Armagh. More, much more, was to come, actions which were saying the Army believed what the IRA was saying and what it intended to do.

This was now the stuff of choreography, words from the IRA, a visible declaration of intent from the British and then decommissioning. It spooked the unionists, but loud and angry responses would not alter the course of events. This was the business of a negotiation that had not involved the DUP, and the party was unable to influence the outcome.

Over the weekend Saturday-Sunday July 30-31, I reported that more of the watchtowers were soon to be dismantled, not just in south Armagh, but in west Belfast and in Derry. At the time of my reporting, I knew much more. I said we should watch for important statements from politicians and security chiefs at the start of next week and that we could expect "angry responses when the full details of what was envisaged are announced". What was expected when those full details emerged was an "earthquake in the unionist community". Before decommissioning, the Army was going to fire the starting pistol for normalisation, a two-year plan to end its support role to the police in Northern Ireland. The Army's decades-long "Operation Banner" was almost as long as the IRA campaign itself. And, in what was now planned, the home-based battalions of the Royal Irish Regiment would be disbanded, and unionists would see this as Ulster soldiers being thrown to the republican wolves. They would see it as another concession to the IRA. Defence Secretary John Reid told Ian Paisley about the plan five minutes after I had reported it on the news. It had come in under the DUP's radar.

On that Saturday and Sunday at the end of July, I had many conversations with senior BBC colleagues in Belfast and elsewhere. There was much planning to be done for this next new day, and big day, in the peace process. I briefed the Belfast editors Andrew Colman, Michael Cairns, Kathleen Carragher and Angelina Fusco and also spoke to Denis Murray, Jon Williams and Mark Simpson, who would be responsible for the London output. This would be one of those stories from Northern Ireland that would have travelling legs. I knew the announcement was planned for midday on Monday, August 1 and, the day before, I filmed in Holywood with my cameraman Nigel Rees. Loyalists were still shooting each other, this time in a feud between the UVF and the LVF, and there was a major security operation in the town. So, I knew my presence with Rees would not raise any suspicions as we filmed the soldiers of the Royal Irish Regiment. They knew nothing of the announcement that would come the following day.

Across the road from them, out of their earshot and in what we call a piece-to-camera, I said that with the announcement on Operation Banner "will come the end of the locally-based Royal Irish Regiment". My reports for Monday were prepared the previous day and, at noon on August 1, the BBC broke the story on the Royal Irish Regiment. This was my news report on *Radio Ulster*.

"The big political and security news in this latest demilitarisation announcement is what's to happen to the Royal Irish Regiment. More than three thousand soldiers serve in what's called the Home Service Battalions with headquarters at Holywood, Omagh and Armagh. But, in moves towards a planned peacetime garrison, these locally based battalions are to go – a long-time republican demand and something which has been announced within days of last Thursday's IRA statement. All of this is part of a plan to end what is called Operation Banner, how the Army describes its support role to the police here, and it will take two years to achieve. Before then, more of the watchtowers are to go, and, within days, we'll see this happen not just in south Armagh but in Derry and west Belfast. On the Falls Road, the Divis Tower is to be demolished. The IRA has ordered an end to its armed campaign and now we're seeing a swift and significant Army response."

About an hour earlier the Secretary of State, Peter Hain, had issued a statement on plans for normalisation, but there was no mention of the Royal Irish Regiment. That hand grenade was thrown in at noon, and it exploded at Stormont where the DUP Assembly party was meeting. By now, I was chatting to David Dunseith on the *Talkback* programme telling him that this was the inevitable military response to the IRA announcement.

Within minutes Jeffrey Donaldson was on the line, and, when he was put through to the studio, he described the latest news, that announcement that the Northern Ireland based Royal Irish Regiment was to be stood down, as a "bombshell". The Lagan Valley MP was at that party meeting at Stormont. The MP Iris Robinson had gone to another office to make a phone call when she heard our news reports. Donaldson told me she called him and that he relayed the information to the meeting. There was then a conversation with Timothy Johnston, the party's director of communications, and the decision was taken to call the *Talkback* programme. Donaldson – a former soldier in the Ulster Defence Regiment – would give the party's initial response to this breaking news.

"The Assembly members were both shocked and angry that the government had not consulted the party before making such a momentous announcement," Donaldson told me.

"They must have known how badly it would have played out in the unionist community. The manner in which the government handled the whole thing significantly damaged relationships between the party and the government."

Donaldson said he believed the decision on the Royal Irish Regiment was "primarily politically motivated". The Army's argument was that this was the inevitable outworking of a new situation.

At two o'clock on the afternoon of August 1, I was at Thiepval Barracks in Lisburn for an interview with Colonel Mark Campbell. The IRA had driven two bombs into this base in October 1996 – its first actions in Northern Ireland after the collapse of the '94 ceasefire. Warrant Officer James Bradwell was injured in the blast and died days later. Now, nine years on inside the same barracks, beside the memorial garden, I was discussing the end of the IRA campaign and the military's response with one of Northern Ireland's most senior soldiers. Colonel Campbell is the commanding officer of the Royal Irish Regiment. We had never met. This interview had been organised through Mervyn Wynne-Jones at the Defence Press Office at Thiepval, and, for the Colonel, it was a day of measured words – a day of thoughtful and careful commentary. Many of his soldiers – just like the DUP – had not yet been told of the decision to disband the locally based battalions of the regiment. They had heard it on the news, and the Army now had a difficult job of internal management on its hands. In our interview I started by asking the Colonel if this was the day that his soldiers had been thrown to the political wolves?

CAMPBELL: No, not at all. I wouldn't accept that. This is clearly a security issue. And we are, we believe, heading towards a point where there has been significant progress in the security of Northern Ireland for the last few years. And our assessment is, particularly following the Provisional IRA statement of last week, that we are approaching a point where the Police Service of Northern Ireland will be able to provide the security and law enforcement to the province without routine military support.

ROWAN: So, do you trust the word of the IRA, if this is to flow so quickly from it?

CAMPBELL: Well, there is a verification process in place, of course. They will have to deliver on their words. But our view is that that is most likely to occur, yes.

ROWAN: Many people will see this as the Royal Irish Regiment being delivered on demand from Sinn Féin.

CAMPBELL: I don't think that's fair. The Royal Irish Regiment and its predecessor, the Ulster Defence Regiment, came into place in 1970, when this was a very dark place. We all remember the violence that was visited upon our community in the 70s, 80s and 90s.

They had a critical role to play and it was very largely because of the Ulster Defence Regiment and the Royal Irish Regiment Home Service that those who would use force to achieve their ends were unable to do so. And I would argue that it is largely because of the commitment of the Ulster Defence Regiment and the Royal Irish Home Service that those who would use force have now turned away from force. And, if you were to say, what was the rationale for forming the Ulster Defence Regiment or the Royal Irish Regiment Home Service, the rationale was really to ensure that democratic politics could prevail in Northern Ireland. That point appears very close. When that occurs, that is an honourable and decent time to conclude the valuable service of the Royal Irish Home Service to this province.

ROWAN: You would accept that there were members of the Royal Irish Regiment and members of the UDR who let the wider regiment down?

CAMPBELL: Yes, that is an interesting point and one that I would have to accept. I would also point out, though, that some fifty thousand people have joined the Royal Irish Regiment and the Ulster Defence Regiment over the period of its existence. There were clearly some bad apples in the barrel and those bad apples sometimes turned to distasteful, despicable terrorist acts. I just wish to reiterate that I and all other members of the regiment utterly condemn those individuals. They let us down, they let society down. And they really needed to get their just desserts in terms of legal process. But, overall, and very significantly, the service of the Royal Irish and Ulster Defence Regiment has been extremely valuable to the province. I think the province owes the regiment – the Ulster Defence Regiment and the Royal Irish – a considerable debt. In fact, I think members of the republican community, they may wish to accept or may well not wish to accept it, also owe a considerable debt. Had they succeeded in achieving their aims through violence I think this would not have been a very pleasant place to live. It is because of the bravery and courage of those who stood and put themselves in harm's way in difficult times that we are where we are today.

ROWAN: You may have heard Martin McGuinness speak yesterday. He talked about the soldiers of the IRA and the soldiers of the British Army beginning to trust each other. He was talking about demilitarisation. Do you think he's got a point?

CAMPBELL: ...We have been raised by a democratic state. We are answerable to a democratic state. We're answerable to rules of engagement and acts of law. I am rather wary of comparing soldiers of the British Army with those who acted outside the law and conducted a vicious campaign on civil society to achieve their aims.

ROWAN: Today is not just about the announcement on the Royal Irish Regiment, it's about steps towards ending Operation Banner – the Army's support role for the police stretching out over many years, put today in some sort of context.

CAMPBELL: Today is an important day and I emphasise that we are now into a two-year process. Verification and so on will need to be undertaken. The Army, this is the longest operational campaign that the British Army has conducted. It has been a difficult campaign. There has been much suffering and much anguish. But it has ultimately been a successful campaign. And I emphasise my point that those who would use violence to achieve political ends have failed to do so. And that those individuals who have now indicated that they're wishing to give up violence have done so in very large measure because their violence was unsuccessful. I'm not talking largely of today. If you think back to the 70s, 80s and 90s, the reason their violence was not successful was not because of diplomacy, was not because of politics, but was because of soldiers – men and women, largely of the UDR and Royal Irish Regiment, who stood in harm's way and did not let those men of violence pass and achieve their aims.

ROWAN: Was it a war with no winners? Did the British Army and the IRA fight each other to a stand still?

CAMPBELL: It's an interesting point. My view is I don't think there's anything to be gained by one side of this province claiming victory over another. I think this province has to be moved forward. I think we need to embrace a bright new democratic future and that will not be assisted by one side claiming victory over another and mud-slinging.

The Colonel was trying to keep things calm. He chose his words in a way not to offend. But inside the unionist, Protestant, loyalist community, the developments of this day were being viewed as yet another concession to republicans. Unionists saw this as an attack by other means, a political assault by the Sinn Féin wing of republicanism that was achieving more than the IRA's years of armed struggle. The bomber Sean Kelly had been released from jail hours before the IRA statement of July 28, and now the Royal Irish Regiment was being disbanded as part of sweeping security changes that had the look of "military Brits out". The question on unionist lips was: What was coming next? In just a few days time there would be another shock to the system – a tremor that went much wider than the unionist community. Three republicans wanted by the Colombian authorities for training Farc guerrillas surfaced in Ireland. The story that James Monaghan, Martin McCauley and Niall Connolly were back broke on RTE News at five o'clock on Friday August 5 – just four days after that announcement on the Royal Irish Regiment. There was no good time for this to happen, but this was a particularly bad time. It didn't matter how it was explained, it didn't matter how much it was said that this was not part of any deal. To unionists it had the look of nod and wink. The three men are wanted on Interpol arrest warrants, they face jail sentences of seventeen years in Colombia, and, now, their presence in Ireland was a political and policing embarrassment. More than that, the timing of all of this was further destabilising the loyalist and unionist communities. This wasn't part of any deal sequence, but try explaining that in those sceptical communities north of the border.

Within weeks we would see an eruption of loyalist violence – linked to a decision not to allow an Orange march to follow its route onto the nationalist Springfield Road. The UDA and the UVF turned on the police and army – there was gunfire, bombs of various descriptions were thrown, and Protestant areas were trashed as loyalists went on a violent rampage. It was a day when Orangemen confronted police officers and soldiers – a day of shame, of serious injuries, of many plastic bullets and of live rounds being returned by police and troops, some of them just back from action in Iraq. This was the storm before a kind of calm. The new IRA watched it all. The IRA no longer engaged in an armed campaign. At interfaces in north, west and east Belfast, senior republicans watched the unfolding madness – watched as loyalists shot themselves in the foot. Away from this scene, other things were happening. The IRA was getting ready for the days of decommissioning that would soon be with us. They were gathering up their guns and explosives. This was the next part of the sequence and General de Chastelain was back in Ireland. On one of those interfaces in Belfast, on September 10, on that day of marching madness and loyalist gunfire, one of those IRA men told me that the story of decommissioning would be behind us by the end of the month. I would speak to him again just sixteen days later.

The DUP knew it was not getting its decommissioning photographs, but it was still trying to insert its chosen church witness into this process. Paisley and his party wanted former Presbyterian Moderator Reverend David McGaughey to be present. He was approached and asked during the negotiations of 2004.

PAISLEY: He would have done it. But he never even was approached by the government. They never even said thank you for the offer.

ROWAN: Did you speak to David McGaughey?

PAISLEY: Oh I did, I spoke to him.

ROWAN: And you were satisfied he would do the job for you?

PAISLEY: Oh yes, he would do the job, well not for me, he would do the job as it should be done… for the people. He would be completely independent. I said to him: 'David, I don't want you to say anything about me. I have nothing to do with it. I'm saying as the largest party in Northern Ireland; we say you're the man to do it. If you can do it, you will help us all.' And he went away and he came back and he said: 'Ian, I will do it'… I took it immediately to the Prime Minister.

ROWAN: But you're saying the government never came back to you to say McGaughey's in or out?

PAISLEY: They never spoke to him.

MARTIN McGUINNESS: He (Paisley) didn't ask us for him (David McGaughey).

ROWAN: At no stage was he… given any impression that McGaughey could be the witness?

McGUINNESS: Absolutely not. One thing about us whenever we deal with negotiations and deal with different aspects of negotiations; if we say we will try for something, we tell people we'll try for it, and when we try for it and we either succeed or we don't succeed, we'll go back right away and we'll say: Well we've got that.

ROWAN: Can you remember off the top of your head if Blair ever asked you could McGaughey be… or the government ever asked you could McGaughey be (a witness)?

McGUINNESS: Well I can't say off the top of my head, but I wouldn't rule out the possibility that at some stage Blair would have said, Ian Paisley would like this guy McGaughey from Kilkeel. But that's an irrelevance, because the fact of the matter was that there was no possibility whatsoever of the IRA agreeing to someone nominated by Ian Paisley.

ROWAN: That was never on?

McGUINNESS: ...someone who was avowedly anti the Good Friday Agreement, ex-member of the RUC, I mean...

ROWAN: It wasn't going to happen?

McGUINNESS: And they knew it wasn't going to happen.

The Reverend McGaughey would not be there. There would be no witness for Paisley, no photographs for Paisley and none of the fine detail of the decommissioning inventory demanded by the DUP. In the week before September 26, the work of decommissioning was done. From early morning to late at night de Chastelain and his colleagues Tauno Nieminen and Andrew Sens counted the guns and weighed the explosives. Everywhere they went they were accompanied by the former President of the Methodist Church, Reverend Harold Good and the Catholic priest Father Alex Reid. In these days, the "decommissioners", the churchmen, and the IRA representative Brian Keenan travelled together in the same vehicle. General de Chastelain assumes they had an "IRA driver". They were at several sites and de Chastelain told me: "We had a feeling that we had covered a large geographical area." When I chatted to him for this book, I asked the general if any photographs had been taken of the decommissioning acts. His answer was clear: "I don't think any photos were taken – absolutely not."

On Sunday, September 25, Aaro Suonio – a Finnish official with the IICD – travelled from Belfast to Dublin. He knew by then that the work of decommissioning had been completed, and he was on his way to meet the three commissioners and to make arrangements for the public presentation of their report the following day. There would be huge interest in this story – a story of those few days in Irish history when the IRA's guns were put away. On Sunday de Chastelain spoke to the governments – his report would officially be presented to them the following day –

and Suonio made arrangements for a news conference in the Culloden Hotel near Holywood, County Down, at two o'clock on Monday, September 26. At just before six on Sunday evening, he called me from Dublin. He told me the IICD would be reporting to the two governments the following morning and that a news conference had been arranged for the afternoon. Minutes later, another source called me with the names of the church witnesses – Harold Good and Alex Reid.

I was able to confirm this with other sources. And, at six o'clock on *Radio Ulster* and on other BBC broadcasts, we were first to run with the news that the story of decommissioning was about to be told, and that it had been witnessed by Reid and Good. This was the first time that Harold Good's name had emerged in public, and he will tell his story in the final chapter of this book – a story of a journey from China to Ireland to watch the IRA put its arms beyond use.

PETER ROBINSON: There was never any problem indicated to us (by the government) in relation to David McGaughey, nor should there be. The fact that he might have been opposed to the Belfast Agreement was in his favour, because to have a witness who might be considered to be sceptical is actually a strength not a weakness. And we are somewhat disturbed to hear from, for instance, Harold Good in recent days that he had been approached right back in November (2004).

Because at no stage was his name (Harold Good) brought to Ian or to myself. We would have been the two closest to the negotiations… Indications were given to us that there didn't appear to be any difficulty with the name … and before the name of David McGaughey was put in by Ian, it was always clear that there would be two clerics – one that we would be appointing and one that they (Sinn Féin) would be appointing… It was expressly indicated that Ian would be nominating the Protestant clergyman. There's no question about that... That's what the government gave us to understand.

This, it seems, was another of the misunderstandings of that long negotiation of 2004 – a negotiation that because of its nature and the fact that much was being channelled through the governments – left room for misinterpretation. But the decommissioning was done now, there could be no action replay, no second chance, and it was done by the IRA in a way that divorced its guns from any future negotiations between republicans and the DUP. Paisley is no longer able to ask for photographs or to name his witness. It happened without pictures and it happened with Harold Good – two facts of life as far as this peace process is concerned; two facts that cannot now be changed. Decommissioning, as far as the IRA is concerned is over. That is accepted by General de Chastelain and by the British and Irish Governments.

A couple of hours before de Chastelain and his colleagues spoke at the Culloden, I was given some indication of what they would say. This was a conversation that confirmed that the commissioners would not be going through the specifics of a decommissioning inventory. But the IICD was working on security estimates of what the IRA had hidden in its bunkers – and I was told that the weaponry that had been put beyond use would correspond to or match those estimates. This would be how the general and his colleagues – Nieminen and Sens – would say that their job had been done:

IICD REPORT: In 2004 the Commission was provided with estimates of the number and quantity of arms held by the IRA. These estimates were produced by the security forces in both jurisdictions and were in agreement. Our inventory (after decommissioning) is consistent with these estimates and we believe that the arms decommissioned represent the totality of the IRA's arsenal. The manner in which the arms were decommissioned is in accordance with the remit given us by the two governments as reflected in their Decommissioning Acts of 1997.

A security estimate given to me by police Special Branch some years ago, and before the decommissioning process began, suggested that the IRA had something in the region of 1700 weapons – a mixture of rifles and handguns – over two tons of the potent explosive Semtex and a mountain of ammunition. Much of what the IRA had concealed in its secret dumps was Libyan-supplied. At the time of its ceasefire all those years ago the IRA had set its face against decommissioning. It talked about "not a bullet, not an ounce", and yet here we where, on September 26, 2005 being told of a belief that every bullet and every ounce had been put beyond use. Decommissioning is unlikely to be that complete, but it is much more significant than many of us had ever thought it would be. On that September day in 2005, as the story of the guns going away unfolded, the different political reactions were much as we expected.

TONY BLAIR: Successive British governments have sought final and complete decommissioning by the IRA for over ten years. Failure to deliver it had become a major impediment to moving forward the peace process. Today it is finally accomplished. And we have made an important step in the transition from conflict to peace in Northern Ireland.

BERTIE AHERN: The IICD statement that the IRA has met its commitments to put all its arms beyond use is of enormous consequence. It is a landmark development; it is of real historic significance; the weapons of the IRA have gone and they're gone in a manner which has been witnessed and verified.

IAN PAISLEY: Instead of openness there was the cunning tactics of a cover-up; the complete failure from General John de

Chastelain to deal with the vital numbers of decommissioning. We do not know how many guns, the amount of ammunition and explosives that were decommissioned. Nor were we told how the decommissioning was carried out.

GERRY ADAMS: I want to commend the leadership of the IRA for moving so decisively. Now, I know that today's announcement will be difficult for republicans. I saw that myself earlier on as we watched the press conference of the IICD and the two independent witnesses. But this was a very brave and a very bold leap and all of us need to think beyond it. We need to think beyond this moment.

MARK DURKAN: Just last February, the IRA warned the Irish people not to underestimate the seriousness of the situation. The Irish people didn't. They stood firm for an end to guns. Now their strong stand has been rewarded. Today's events also demonstrate the utter futility of violence. Violence never won anything in the North. Violence does not pay. It costs. In lives lost, in economies ruined, in communities wrecked. That's something that so many victims of the Troubles know too well. Today as we look forward, we must not leave them behind – isolated and forgotten.

SIR REG EMPEY: Clearly it would appear that a significant development in terms of decommissioning has taken place. However we regret that once again, this development has failed to maximise public confidence… It is imperative that not only arms are decommissioned but that the dismantling of the Republican movement's criminal empire is also completed… This move by republicans should illicit a response from loyalist paramilitaries who said that if the IRA decommissioned that they would follow suit.

Paisley's party was the most negative in the various responses to decommissioning. It had not been as the DUP leader had wanted it, but it had been better than many had ever thought possible.

The "talking eyes" of Harold Good and Alex Reid had added to the credibility of these final acts of putting arms beyond use, but just days later, Reid would find himself at the centre of a major controversy when, during an angry exchange, he compared the unionist treatment of the nationalist community to Nazism. There will, of course, be continuing arguments about what is meant by "total" decommissioning. I have said I don't believe there is such a thing. But what would be the consequences of IRA guns surfacing in the future? The DUP knows the answer to that question. A few weeks after the de Chastelain statement, I spoke to the party's deputy leader Peter Robinson.

ROBINSON: From all accounts the process seems to have been that the IRA had nine decommissioning sites. They asked all of their quartermasters through various units to bring their weaponry to one of those nine sites. I think in probably virtually every case the local IRA have held something back in reserve. They've probably given them all of the weaponry that has forensic attached to it. So, they've kept themselves clean equipment. But we are getting reports from within the security forces of their belief that weapons have been held back. Only time will tell the extent to which they have done it. Mind you, politically, if those guns ever come out or if they're ever found there would be a massive problem for the Republican movement, because their leadership has staked its reputation on all of the weapons having gone. But time alone will tell what the real story is. But the purpose of decommissioning, because we always knew that they could improvise weapons or they could buy new weapons in, the purpose of decommissioning was always to build confidence in the community that the guns have gone for good.

ROWAN: Do you think leaving McGaughey out was a major mistake?

ROBINSON: You look at it from the point of view of: Where

would the Democratic Unionist Party have been if McGaughey had been in? The Democratic Unionist Party would have met with McGaughey, he was their choice, they would clearly have taken his word, and you would have had a far more favourable response to it as a result of our witness having witnessed it.

Coming up to one o'clock on Monday September 26, I answered my mobile phone to P O'Neill. We had a brief conversation in which he dictated a short statement to me and then asked me to read it back to him. This was a check for accuracy.

IRA STATEMENT: The leadership of Oglaigh na hEireann announced on July 28 that we had authorised our representative to engage with the IICD to complete the process to verifiably put arms beyond use. The IRA leadership can now confirm that the process of putting our arms beyond use has been completed. P O'Neill.

The first call I ever took from P O'Neill – a different "P O'Neill" at that time – was after the slaughter of the Enniskillen bomb in 1987. None of us could see a ceasefire back then, none of us were even thinking about decommissioning. No one had ever spoken the words arms beyond use. There have been many IRA statements in that period 1987-2005 – statements of killing and crisis of hope and despair. Brian Keenan first spoke to General de Chastelain in December 1999. In the six years since, they talked and didn't talk. Decommissioning happened and then didn't happen – a consequence of the deals and no deals within the political process.

But the Army General and the IRA's military man finally got the job done. Others saw it through those "talking eyes" that the former Presbyterian Moderator Ken Newell had said would bring something more to the process of decommissioning than a "silent

NO GUNS, NOW GOVERNMENT?

photograph", and Newell for one has been convinced by what has happened:

"I honestly do believe that it was momentous, it was major, it was significant and it was final. I think that there are certain questions that remain outstanding, but I don't think there's anybody on the earth who can answer them."

That killing statement by the IRA in 1987 seems a very long time ago. We are in a new and different situation now, in which we may have heard the last words of this war from P O'Neill. Martin McGuinness believes the IRA is now out of the equation. That means that P O'Neill signed off with that statement that the guns are gone. Now, this process waits for the loyalists and watches for the outcome of different consultations that are going on inside that community. Can the UDA, the UVF and the Red Hand Commando first silence their guns and then match the IRA's decommissioning? This will be the new focus of the arms process – the new work for de Chastelain and the other men of decommissioning. The phase of "not a bullet, not an ounce" has passed, and we have had the ending of the armed campaign and the decommissioning of the guns.

CHAPTER SIX

THE "PROD" PROBLEM

"People were looking to the future and 'crystal balling' and knew the IRA, in order to get from Position A to Position B, would have to move massively... We knew that the IRA was positioning itself to decommission substantial chunks of its arsenal in order to gain political office – ministerial seats." Senior UVF leader, October 2005, on why loyalists began talking about the future of their organisations.

"I believe the threat of the IRA has gone away with one proviso. I think that the history of the IRA – and some of us in the loyalist community understand the IRA very well and their history – the IRA, I imagine, would never want to leave themselves in the position of I Ran Away. So, I imagine they will have catered for that." Loyalist politician David Ervine, October 2005, commenting on the IRA's decision to end its armed campaign and to decommission its weapons.

"That's the best way to describe it (inevitable). He was probably the most hated man in Belfast, certainly on the loyalist side. The organisation (the UDA) will be the automatic suspects. He should have been away – out of sight and out of mind." UDA leader, October 2005, commenting on the murder of the paramilitary "brigadier" Jim Gray.

"Over recent years the confidence of loyalist communities has been

*weakened by internal feuding indulged in by all as well as
criminality which has dishonoured the memory of our fallen
comrades."* LVF leadership statement, October 30, 2005.

OCTOBER 12, 1994. The three men in the room were members of
the loyalist paramilitary leadership – some of the most senior
figures in the Ulster Volunteer Force, the Red Hand Commando
and the Ulster Defence Association. At the time, they were
speaking as representatives of a Combined Loyalist Military
Command, and, on that night in October 1994, we were on the
eve of their ceasefire announcement. Two of the three men I met
back then are still in positions of leadership; the third was ousted
in an internal coup within the UDA. One of those who later
replaced him was John Gregg – who became a paramilitary
"brigadier". He is dead now – murdered by rival loyalists in one
of the many feuds that have been fought inside this community
in recent years. The UDA, the UVF, the linked Red Hand
Commando and the Loyalist Volunteer Force have all been
involved. There is no longer a threat to loyalism from the IRA,
but loyalists are a threat to themselves, and we have watched them
turn their guns on each other – shoot each other dead and shoot
themselves in the foot. Gregg and Jim Gray were members of
what the UDA calls an "Inner Council". They were murdered by
members of that paramilitary group. Later, Gray's killing was
described as "the tying up (of) loose ends". In other infighting, at
another time, a leader in the Loyalist Volunteer Force, Stephen
Warnock, was shot dead by the Red Hand Commando, and one
of the most senior figures in that organisation, Jim Johnston, was
murdered in a revenge attack.

This is but the tip of the loyalist iceberg. Others are living in
exile, among them Johnny Adair, a one-time Shankill UDA
leader, who for years directed and led the murderous activities of
that organisation. The ceasefire of 1994 was disciplined. It
survived the IRA attack in Canary Wharf and the bombing of the

Army's Headquarters at Thiepval Barracks in Lisburn. But there have been periods since when the loyalists have lost all discipline, and, when those looking in on them, have lost all hope. Today, there is no rush to decommission and there is a struggle to convince people that the Provos haven't won and the Prods haven't been sold out. The paramilitaries in this community have on occasions trampled all over their political representatives. Gary McMichael and David Adams were victims of such treatment, and there have been times when loyalism has looked leaderless and hopeless.

We hear from them that the peace process has pandered to the "Provos"; that the loyalists have been left behind. We hear too of social deprivation and of people in this community feeling like second class citizens. But the loyalists have at times destroyed their own communities – plagued their own people and polluted the places where they live with drugs. They have trampled their own reputation into the ground. All of the above is "the Prod problem", and the challenge for the political and paramilitary leaderships in this community is to point it back in the direction of the peace process.

"There are some of the young lads in the organisation want to go back to 1974 – bring the country to a standstill because they think we are being sold out, and I'm trying to convince them that that's not the way to go, explaining all the problems with that," said Jackie McDonald, one of the most senior figures in the loyalist leadership.

"Loyalism for a while; we used to ask: Do you want us to be good or do you want us to be bad? And, for a while, I thought they wanted us to be good; they paid us a certain amount of lip service. Now I just believe… they just want us to be bad. They've decided that we are easier dealt with if we are bad. There have been so many feuds, so much infighting, that they can turn round and say: What threat are they to anybody only themselves? Loyalists have to rise above that."

Privately, quietly, the thinking loyalists will acknowledge the significance of the IRA statement of July 2005 and the decommissioning that followed – decommissioning which one senior paramilitary figure described as "substantial but not total". You will not convince anyone in the loyalist community that the IRA has rid itself of all its weapons – in the same way that the UVF, UDA and Red Hand Commando will always have what they feel they need to defend their community and defend themselves. This is still a place where people take comfort in the gun. But, again, the thinking loyalists recognise the significance and symbolism of the IRA decommissioning that has happened, and they recognise too the political and strategic compromises made by republicans. The big question now is: How do you solve that Prod problem? Two of the three men who sat in that room with me on the Shankill Road in October 1994 have turned their minds to doing just that. For a long time it was hard to see what they were up to. It was hidden behind that feuding and infighting. It was out of our vision and their secret, private, talking was being drowned out by the gunfire. In 2004 – in the period of that negotiation involving the governments, the DUP and Sinn Féin – the UVF and the Red Hand Commando began talking to their organisations.

"It began that consultation process in the absolute knowledge that the IRA was going to do what the IRA has done," said David Ervine, the only loyalist survivor in the political mainstream. He knows the men who are directing that loyalist consultation and knows the intended outcome.

"They were aware that it (the IRA's decisions) would change the *raison d'être*, and they went through a consultation process which was saying: What about us if this happens? It is a process of scenario building, in the event that this happens, that happens, and certainly at least one of those questions was (what happens) when the IRA decommission and change mode?"

I have been asked many times by many people in recent

months what loyalism needs, and I have answered, that part of it, politically speaking, needs to be "talked to" and the other part of it, security speaking, needs to be sorted. The men of the room of 1994 are still worth talking to, and there are others in leadership positions in different organisations who are genuinely trying to stabilise the loyalist community. Their enemies come from within.

They are figures in key positions in the paramilitary leadership who have been the destroyers of the reputation of loyalism as well as the destroyers of lives. Adair is one such figure. Jim Gray was another, and there are more.

The UDA's north Belfast "brigadier" Andre Shoukri is considered by many to be a destabilising influence, and those who know him say he could turn out to be "worse" than Adair.

Loyalism needs sound guidance and advice, and its leadership needs people who will ask the tough question – people from both inside and outside the paramilitaries. A Loyalist Commission, made up of those paramilitaries as well as church people and community figures, was meant to do just that, but it has failed, or certainly that is the perception of it from outside loyalism. And now the "war makers" of the UVF and the Red Hand Commando are trying again to be the "peace makers". They are about to be asked some of the biggest questions of their leadership reign. Their authority and influence will be tested, and the challenge to them is to re-invent and then re-deliver the loyalism of 1994. But first there were matters to be settled, one of them being the continued existence of the LVF, which has been blamed – accurately it has to be said – for many of the feuds. During the writing of this book, the organisation issued a statement standing down its "military units". It said this was "a direct response to recent IRA actions and statements". But that was only part of the story. The organisation had been under attack from the UVF, and while the LVF said it was leaving the stage "not from a position of weakness or under threat", the reality was that it was pushed from that stage, that it was left with no choice. As for the mainstream loyalist leadership – including the UVF and the Red Hand Commando – it will have a lot of convincing to do before it will be believed. Some organisations are "specified", meaning that their ceasefires are no longer recognised by the government. The most recent feud killings, followed by attacks on the security forces in early September 2005, left the Northern Ireland Secretary of State Peter Hain with only one choice to make. But the feuding is only part of the loyalist story. The consultation offers up other possibilities but no "quick fixes". In October 2005, I spoke to David Ervine.

ERVINE: Loyalism has had its focus diverted (by the feuding) but it has still always been hankering, if you like, to get back to the big picture. And the big picture is about paramilitaries going off the stage, and they know that only too well. So, one is buoyed by the fact that they have been going through the consultation process. If I had to call it, I would say they are half way through it.

ROWAN: Because you've got the same leadership by and large as you had in 1994; ceasefire delivered in 1994, ceasefire disciplined through Canary Wharf, and then people have this view, perception, that loyalists fell into a deep hole. Is it trying to climb back out again?

ERVINE: Well I think we have to set a context of what you've just said. If you look across the vista from 1997, the restoration of the IRA ceasefire after Canary Wharf; if we talk about it in structured terms, the IRA have not attacked for political purposes since that time. So against the backdrop where the enemy is quiet, we've got loyalism looking as if it's all over the place, and you're right, the question is why would the same leadership be behaving this way when it was clearly very, very favourably impressed by the opportunity of exploration? Why? And I think therein lies a series of questions. I'll constantly be accused of being a conspiracy theorist... but I don't think it was by accident that a lot of that stuff happened. My sense though, now, is the disruption within loyalism is going to diminish... the battle going on within loyalism is unsustainable certainly from the point of view of the broader society's attitudes to it and indeed, I have to say to you, the paramilitarists that I talk to are sickened by it.

Those paramilitarists, as Ervine describes them, are the leaders of the UVF and Red Hand Commando – the men who are managing that debate inside their organisations and who are trying to concentrate the minds of their membership on a series of questions set out in a three-page document. But the backdrop to that consultation is a mood in the wider unionist community, that in terms of concessions, republicans are winning.

ROWAN: Do you accept that the biggest threat to the loyalist community at this stage is from within the loyalist community?
ERVINE: Yes; without question. Also I would say to you with some, I hope, logic attached to it; the biggest threat outside the loyalist community to the loyalist community is from unionist leadership, and that unionist leadership really does need to wake up and give people hope rather than this constant sense of dismay... If unionism is prepared to change the message, it means that they are prepared to truck with republicans. Once you are prepared to truck with the republicans, then the republicans can never play any games around the notion that unionists will never give them a place in the sun and there's still a battle for equality going on, and the spin-off from that is that the challenge to them (republicans) is to do business with us.

In October 2005, eleven years on from the ceasefire announcement of the Combined Loyalist Military Command, I met again with one of the men who was in the room that night in

1994 – one of the men who was key to that announcement back then, and whose voice will matter most in this latest loyalist consultation. This time we met in east Belfast. My source for this conversation is the UVF's most senior leader – its only "brigadier". It was he who told me that this talking process was not about producing a "quick fix". At this stage the leadership was not "laying it down as it is" – the consultation was about talking and listening. That talking and listening was across a range of issues; the future role of both the UVF and the Red Hand Commando, how those organisations are viewed within their own community, why they are still recruiting, the consequences of members being involved in criminal activities including drugs, and the question of dialogue, including the possibility of direct talks with republicans.

On the issue of recruitment, that internal three-page consultation document asks two questions: Why ten years into a ceasefire is the UVF numerically stronger than in 1994? Why has there been continued large-scale recruitment post ceasefire?

"We need to look at recruitment in the light of other people (the IRA) leaving the stage; not only recruitment but membership," the UVF's most senior leader told me.

The issue here is about ending recruitment and about standing down and sending home those men who are no longer needed in the loyalist war with the IRA. The UVF's consultation document accepts that "the major republican threat (has) gone". But the discussion on recruitment and membership needs to go wider than the UVF and the Red Hand Commando. My source said there would have to be an agreement or understanding that these people would not be picked up in the nets of the other loyalist organisations. He told me the UVF leadership was "mindful of the discipline" that the IRA had shown since its ceasefire. All of the stuff of its "armed struggle" – attacks on the security forces, on economic targets and on the loyalist/unionist community had ended.

But the "unarmed struggle" was a different matter, and, here, he is talking about community interface tensions, mostly in Belfast and related to contentious parades – those parades I mentioned earlier in the book at Ardoyne and Whiterock.

"What we are telling our grassroots is that we need to move to a position of unarmed resistance," my source said.

It is on these interface issues, that the UVF leadership would see benefit in a direct dialogue with republicans. In its consultation paper, under a heading – Engagement with Republicans – the following points are made:

- Should the organisation engage directly in challenging the enemy through dialogue?
- Are we losing out by not doing so?
- What are the possible benefits?
- What are the drawbacks/dangers?
- If we don't challenge them (republicans) face-to-face, who will?
- Is it right that those who sat on the sidelines of armed resistance for years should engage on our behalf?
- Is it right that those who took up the cause of armed resistance should be marginalised and demonised by politicians and civic leaders who never took part in the physical war?

"Our leadership (UVF-Red Hand Commando) would see our combatants having been involved in the conflict for almost 40 years – you are talking about 1966. Why should the pitch be abandoned by them at this stage and given to (others) not involved in the conflict."

That question posed by the UVF's most senior leader raises the possibility that some of those who fought the "war" with republicans are now thinking about how they best make peace, starting at the interfaces and working up, and that is another indication of a loyalist acceptance that the IRA has now gone away.

"We can sit down and look those boys in the eye, (and say) this is the consequence, and you get more done that way."

This is the loyalists thinking of a dialogue in which the "fighters" are of equal weight. In other words they are getting ready to do their own talking with republicans rather than have it done through the voices of church or community or political representatives. And this is one of the new possibilities in the era beyond the IRA's statement and its acts of decommissioning.

On paper, and in what we are listening to around this consultation inside the UVF and the Red Hand Commando, you would have to say: It reads and sounds well. But, at this stage, all we have to judge it on are the questions that are being asked. We don't yet have the answers. We can read in the three-page consultation document what the mind of the leadership is, but what about the members. Will they listen? Is it possible, eleven years on, to re-deliver the loyalism of 1994? And have those who have survived in leadership positions still got the necessary influence and authority to put and take their organisations through another significant process of change? This will be the real test of this consultation – to match the words with appropriate actions or inaction. On this, the political jury will have to be persuaded in the final submissions whenever they come. But the UVF/Red Hand Commando is but one part of a complex loyalist community. The largest of the paramilitary organisations is the Ulster Defence Association. It has been brought back in from the political cold. Its ceasefire has been recognised since November 2004, and there has been a political engagement since then, including a meeting with Tony Blair's Chief of Staff Jonathan Powell at Stormont. In the early weeks of 2005, he met the Inner Council of that time, as it pushed to get itself inside Downing Street.

That hasn't happened yet, and, less than a year after its ceasefire was again recognised, the UDA is the main suspect in the murder of Jim Gray, who was shot dead in October 2005. Gray was one of those who had met Powell.

Just weeks later, the entire UDA organisation turned against him as it has turned against others in the past, including Johnny Adair. This is the familiar world of loyalism – where you can be a leader one day and an outcast the next. Adair is living in exile and Gray is dead. At one time, both were "brigadiers" in the UDA – members of a so-called Inner Council. It was that Inner Council – the top tier of the UDA leadership – that issued a statement on March 30 2005 saying that Gray and other leaders of the organisation in east Belfast had been "stood down". As they say in these parts, the writing was on the wall. Like Adair, Gray was a public embarrassment – a loyalist of considerable wealth, a loyalist who was both a drug user and a drug dealer, a loyalist who would not have been in the trenches during those days of "war" in Ulster, and a loyalist whose only interest was self-interest. His nickname was "Doris Day". He drove a fancy car, had blonde hair and an all-year tan. He liked pink jumpers, white trousers and he always dripped in gold. He was one of those loyalists who was more interested in his bank balance than he was in the state of the Union, and he was one of those destroyers of the loyalist reputation and the loyalist community. Inside the world in which he lived, he had crossed the line.

Soon after he was "stood down", Gray was arrested. His finances were being investigated, but he was given bail, and on October 4 he was shot dead at his father's home. Only about a dozen people turned up for his funeral – another example of how the mighty fall inside this loyalist world. Hours after the killing, I spoke to one of the men who sat on that Inner Council with Gray. There was no sympathy. I asked him if the killing was inevitable, and he told me that was the best way to describe it. He accepted that the UDA – an organisation supposedly on ceasefire – would be the "automatic suspects" when it came to putting a label on the shooting. Gray, he said, "was probably the most hated man in Belfast – certainly on the loyalist side", and he had "signed his own death warrant".

"It was just one of those tying-up a few loose ends, if you like.

I couldn't believe… I thought he would have had the sense to take himself away out of the road. To try to come and live in the middle of east Belfast after torturing and tormenting those people for years; and he still did it even when he got out. He was abusing people in the street and saying things like, from what I'm led to believe: 'I'm Jim Gray. I don't do what anybody tells me. Who's going to bother me?' He just invited it. He literally asked for it."

His death was celebrated with a bonfire, and, beside it, loyalists painted the words "Rest in Pink".

"Members of the organisation actually went to the people and said: That's in bad taste. And they said: Don't you tell us. That man put us through hell and we want to do this."

My source said: "I don't blame anybody if they suspect the organisation – (the UDA)."

There was no hiding from this particular whodunit. It was much too obvious to be denied. And, here again, we had another example of just how loud the loyalist guns can be.

The big focus just a few days earlier when General de Chastelain reported the completion of the IRA's decommissioning process was on how "total" that had been. But, as I write, none of the main loyalist organisations has put a single gun beyond use, not one gun or bullet has been decommissioned by the UVF, the UDA or the Red Hand Commando – the organisations of that Combined Loyalist Military Command which first delivered the ceasefire of October 1994. They are not firing their weapons at the nationalist community now, nor can they pretend to be at war with republicans. But they are using their guns on each other, and, as they start to accept that the threat of the IRA has gone away or is going away, so they need to begin to think about how they give reassurance to each other. But you won't hear any of that in these comments on decommissioning from one of the UDA's most senior leaders:

"It's not even being considered really because of the way loyalism is being treated. And, at the end of the day, it's for the same reasons that the 'Provies' haven't decommissioned all their gear. Loyalism won't do it either, because drug dealers are going to be the problem a year or two down the road, and they certainly aren't going to decommission anything. (And then you have) the good guys and the bad guys – republicans or loyalists. There is going to be people expelled from the loyalist organisations, but some of these people will have access to the weapons, and they'll take the weapons with them. So, the good guys; they have to hold onto the weapons to deal with the bad guys. So, there's not going to be a lot left in the middle to decommission."

Loyalism needs to be joined up again as it was more than a decade ago. It needs to think collectively as it did a decade ago and it needs the same sort of decision-making and decision-enforcing approach that it had back then. That is the last time that the loyalist paramilitaries had some standing and some respect in this process. And that was because they showed themselves capable not only of delivering a ceasefire but adhering to it.

Solving "the Prod problem" is entirely possible. So much of it is of their own making, and so much of it is the stuff of paranoia. The Provos haven't won and nor have the loyalists lost. There have been significant compromises by republicans. The decommissioning of the IRA has dwarfed the very little that has happened on the loyalist side. Only a very few guns have been given up, not by the UDA, the UVF or the Red Hand Commando, but by the Loyalist Volunteer Force. And as for the sweeping security changes that are now being planned – as part of ending "Operation Banner" – these are a natural military response to the IRA leaving the stage. The loyalists are still on it – and it was they who were attacking the security forces in September of 2005, when we heard the guns and the bombs of the UDA and the UVF. But now we see some of the leaders of 1994 starting to assert themselves again – quietly in the background in that consultation which aims to take loyalism back into this peace process. As one paramilitary leader said to me: "We're all about to get a second bite of the cherry."

Before then, David Ervine believes that not just the loyalist leadership, but the unionist leadership also, has to act in a way that changes the atmosphere across the Protestant community. He also believes it inevitable that Ian Paisley and Sinn Féin will end up in government together.

ERVINE: There will be a Sinn Féin – DUP government and, I have to say to you, if there isn't, unionism will lose out massively again. There really is nowhere to go here. You can raise barriers all day and all night. You can keep telling your people the bad news as you see it – bad people in government, no guns-no government, and all of the negatives that stop logical politics taking place here…

In the event of no Northern Ireland Assembly, the direct rule process, I think, takes on a new dimension, and there is no such thing, I think, any more, whether I like it or whether I don't, of a direct rule that doesn't in some way route some of the material through Dublin… And if I'm right, that unionism has nowhere to go, he's (Paisley is) in pole position. He has to do the business… even though people believe he is culturally incapable of doing the deal… I think the British Government will create a construct, the DUP will go in squealing and yelling, but, meanwhile, back at the ranch, they'll do the business.

The senior loyalist leader Jackie McDonald also believes this to be inevitable.

ROWAN: Do you think there is an inevitability that Paisley will come to do business with the Provos?

McDONALD: He has to… I think that some day they have to get there. And although I don't like it and the loyalist people won't like it, that's democracy. They've (the DUP) got the mandate, and the "Shinners" have got the mandate, and they're going to sit down and talk. I think they have to.

ROWAN: Do you think loyalists will have to talk to republicans eventually?

McDONALD: If the "Big Man" (Paisley) does it, or the DUP does it, you know, the world starts tomorrow.

First, the loyalist world has to change. Their political project of 1994 and before, which showed some early promise, has been all but destroyed – a self-destruction by the loyalist paramilitaries. The UVF leader who I met in 1994 and then again in October 2005 during my research for this book, is one of those who could change things. He sings in tune with Ervine and McDonald and believes it inevitable that political business will be done between the DUP and Sinn Féin, and that Paisley will have his "prize" as First Minister. But he must also know that if loyalism wants to be a part of that political future, then it must change and change quickly. That large-scale recruitment into the paramilitary organisations will have to end. The feuding cannot continue, nor can the criminality. The man who leads the UVF says he wants to change things, but he is not interested in cosmetic change:

"What is the point of going in for grand gestures on decommissioning? What we are trying to do is decommission the mindsets first."

That would be a start – a beginning of some addressing of "the Prod problem" – an addressing of this conflict inside the loyalist head. Do they want to be a part of the political and peace processes as they were in 1994, or do they want to believe that they are being sold out to the Provos? The loyalist leadership has that decision to make.

In November 2005 Andre Shoukri appeared in court on blackmail, intimidation and money-laundering charges. A detective told the court that the loyalist had replied "Not guilty" when the charges were put to him.

CHAPTER SEVEN

LAST WORDS

"Someone who has lost a loved one and for whom no one has ever been brought to account feels that evidence has been destroyed along with the weapons. I can understand that, but there is a hard decision to be made there. In destroying the weapons, you have destroyed the possibility of another victim... You save a life. Retaining it (the weapon) will not bring back the life of the lost loved one, but by destroying it, you're destroying the possibility of it ever being used again on another person. And, so, you're hopefully ensuring the safety of other lives. So those are the hard decisions that have to be made and those are the choices." Decommissioning witness Reverend Harold Good, speaking October 15, 2005.

CHINA, SEPTEMBER 2005. It was a secret that had travelled with him on a journey of many thousand miles; one of those stories of the peace process that could not be told, not even among close and trusted friends. Harold Good had known that these days were coming – days when he would be in the company of the IRA and those others tasked with the job of decommissioning. He had had time to prepare, to think through what he was being asked to do and to get himself ready to carry the heavy weight that was about to be placed on his shoulders. For months he had known that he was to be the Protestant church witness to the IRA's decommissioning. He was to be those "talking eyes" that Ken Newell referred to earlier in this book. Good is a former Methodist President, a man whose church work placed him on the loyalist Shankill Road in Belfast in those dark days of the early Troubles; and, now, here he was, in a situation where he could see the light of some sort of ending.

The churchman was in China, but he was needed back in Ireland. Good had first been approached in November 2004 by a person he will only describe as being "intimately involved in the peace process". There was no certainty at this time that decommissioning was definitely going to happen. The DUP, Sinn Féin and the two governments were still negotiating. But the story had already emerged that new church witnesses had been agreed, and Good was being approached , I suppose, on the basis of "just in case". In how things developed, he would not be needed until September 2005, but, by the time he was asked again, he had already committed himself to lead a group of church friends on "a journey of understanding" to China. His wife Clodagh was with him – the only one in a group of forty and more who knew why her husband had to leave.

"I had to explain to my group that I had to come back (to Ireland) and asked them to trust me, that there was a good reason for my coming back without telling them what that reason was."

In October 2005, just a couple of weeks after that decommissioning job had been completed, I chatted to Harold Good at his home just outside Holywood in County Down. He spoke quietly. Indeed, he almost whispered his words into my tape recorder. It was as if he was still in that moment back in September, that moment that required so much secrecy – that moment when he watched the arms of the IRA being put out of use. Even the bits that he could tell were told in a guarded, cautious and careful way. Every word had to be measured.

"Honour is something which goes beyond what you write on paper. Trust goes beyond a contract. It is something that you know within yourself that you must respect and honour. And as people respected me for my role, I can do no less than respect what would be their wishes."

His journey of understanding in China took him on a detour – through Shanghai airport, back to Ireland, into a religious shop where he picked up a bundle of prayers and then into the company of the IRA, the three decommissioning commissioners and Father Alex Reid, the second of the church witnesses. In that religious shop, Good had chosen the prayer of Saint Francis of Assisi:

> *Lord make me an instrument of your peace.*
> *Where there is hate, let me sow love.*
> *Where there is injury, pardon,*
> *Where there is doubt, faith,*
> *Where there is despair, hope,*
> *Where there is darkness, light and where there is sadness, joy.*
> *O Divine Master, grant that I may not so much seek to be consoled,*
>   *as to console.*
> *To be understood, as to understand;*
> *To be loved, as to love;*
> *For it is in giving that we receive –*
> *It is in pardoning that we are pardoned;*
> *And it is in dying that we are born to eternal life.*

As a parting gift he gave a copy of the prayer to those he met during those days of decommissioning – to de Chastelain and his colleagues, to Father Alex Reid and the IRA representatives.

When I met Harold Good in his home, there were many things I wanted to talk about and many things I knew he could not tell. We each understood that.

"I think the detail is secondary – it's interesting, very interesting – and there might come a time when I can give a little more detail. But, at the moment, I am conscious of the trust that has been invested in me, and it may well be that others want to invest trust in me for some other purpose or reason. So, I'm most anxious to neither say nor do anything which could in anyway be construed as a betrayal of trust."

I suppose these were the ground rules for our conversation, but there was a lot he could talk about – the approach that was made to him, the secret he had to carry, sharing that secret with his wife Clodagh, his journey to China and back, meeting the IRA and watching it destroy its weaponry, and, then the coming back and the telling of what could be told. What now follows is what Harold Good was able to tell me about all of those things.

GOOD: We stated publicly that Father Alex Reid and myself were approached separately – individually and separately – by somebody intimately involved in the peace process, asking, if asked would we be prepared to act in this way. And I can't speak for Alex Reid but I know what I said was that I would have to be assured that I was acceptable to a range of people – not any one group of people, who were directly or indirectly involved in this process. And I said I would have to be assured of that because I don't want to put myself into a situation where I would not be acceptable to people who need persuasion. And I was revisited by the same person saying soundings have been taken and that I could be assured that from those soundings my concerns could be met – that I would be acceptable… Now, there was no letter of appointment, I don't use the word appoint, I never said we were appointed but what I was being made aware of was that I would be acceptable.

ROWAN: When was this, Harold?

GOOD: That would have been late November of last year prior to what was expected to take place last December – sometime in November when I was first approached… I think it was in my home.

ROWAN: You were assured that if you were to take up the role that people would be confident in what you said.

GOOD: Yes, I was given to understand that I was acceptable to a range of people – people who would have to have confidence in me and therefore in what I would say.

ROWAN: You made clear at your news conference that you were not appointed by the IRA, and there is this confusion, this misunderstanding, about that still. Just explain that clearly.

GOOD: I've just said that I wasn't appointed by the IRA. What I'm saying is that I was given to understand that I would be acceptable to a range of people, and obviously they (the IRA) would have been included within that range of people to whom I would be acceptable and who would have confidence in me as being trustworthy and that whatever I would say at the end of this exercise, people could find me believable and would have confidence in my integrity. That is what I had to bring to the exercise.

ROWAN: So just to be absolutely clear, when you were approached by that person intimately involved in peace work here, they were not approaching you on behalf of the IRA?

GOOD: Not directly, no. I'm sure this person was in touch with lots of people. I just don't want to go there. As soon as I start going there, we start into the business of the game of elimination; was it this person or that person, and I just don't want to go there. It was somebody who obviously was well placed to be in touch with the folks who needed some help in this direction to find folks who would be acceptable to a range of people.

ROWAN: December then didn't happen; the deal didn't happen at that stage, I assume things went very quiet for a while.

GOOD: Very quiet – heard nothing for a long time… I didn't even know whether or not I would be approached again… (and then) I was approached again some time late summer.

ROWAN: After the IRA statement of July?

GOOD: It was after the IRA statement of July, it would have been following that, following that statement, that I would have been approached – following the July statement.

ROWAN: So you knew you were going to be a witness, you knew you were going to be someone who had to testify to the IRA's guns being put beyond use, what kind of thoughts went through your head at that stage?

GOOD: First thing I did was ask my wife, Clodagh. I asked her. She's an interesting person, her politics, I always say she's highly political without realising it, because she wants to know if the buses are running, is there good health care for us and for our children and their children, she wants to know are the bins going to be emptied on Thursday, is the pension going to be there on Tuesday, all the things that really matter, and she's less concerned about who's actually making all those things happen, as long as they happen. And I keep saying, would that we are all as politically astute, and she would say that she has no interest in politics... She's hugely supportive of anything I do and have done, hugely supportive... So, (I said) I need to know that you're comfortable with this, and she said to me, I think you should do it because this could be a completion for things that you have longed for, asked for, prayed for and put in your twopence-worth over the years with others, and she said I think you should do it and there could be a completion, and that word, completion, is a big word for me... There was no way I could say no.

ROWAN: What can you tell me about the moment you left your home, the thought that went through your head at that stage, what you said to your wife as you left?

GOOD: Let me tell you it was much more complicated than that. I had arranged to take forty-one people with me to China in the middle of September and it clashed with the dates that others wanted this exercise to happen...Here I was with forty-one people all signed up to go on this. I lead these, what I call, journeys of understanding... So, what do I do? I said: 'Well, look, I really am stuck here. I think you should find someone else, because I'm just not going to be available if it (decommissioning) has to be done within a timescale.' And they said: No. The word I got was, you're the person the people want to be involved in this, you're the person who's trusted, and we're not going looking elsewhere. So, there was a bit of, shall we say, accommodating of each other, and the accommodation was that I could go to China – that I would go. I mean there was no way I was going to have to seek permission to go to China. I was committed, but that I would return after a week. I would get them started on their journey, and that I would then hand over the leadership to one of my group. That I would return. So, I had to explain to my group that I had to come back, and asked them to trust me that there was a good reason for my coming back without telling them what that reason was... They would have been all church people from as far away as Kerry – Kerry to Belfast and everything in between. So I flew back from Shanghai on my own, left them all in China and arrived back into this exercise, and it was pretty well straight into it upon my arrival back.

So it was a kind of strange thing just to be leading people there, the comfort of all those folks and your wife, abandoning her and them in the middle of China and coming back on one's own...

ROWAN: So your wife was part of that group in China, and she obviously was the one who did know why you were coming back?

GOOD: She was the one who knew why I was coming back.

ROWAN: What were her last words; can you remember what her last words were as you left China?

GOOD: Be careful, take care, and I said: 'I'll be OK'. She obviously like anybody else would wonder: What is decommissioning actually all about, are you going to be at risk? She would be very concerned, and it was asking a lot of her because, I knew, when you're in a situation you know, I was going to say you know where you are, but I'm not sure that that was totally true, but you know what I mean. It reminded me of dark days and nights in the early part of the Troubles when I would have been around the Shankill trying to be helpful to people in that awful situation in those dark days and nights, when I would be out all night, poor Clodagh would be sitting at home lying in bed not having an idea. We didn't have mobile phones in those days, so, she wouldn't have known where I was. I knew I was alright but she'd no means for knowing I was alright, and there were nights when there were radio reports of people being shot and all this kind of thing. I don't want to be melodramatic about that, but I imagine for her it was a little bit like reliving something of that, not knowing where I was, and who I was with and what it entailed, and she was away thousands of miles away in China, in a room on her own at nights and then arriving back in Ireland and still not knowing where I was because I was out of communication during that period.

ROWAN: The job hadn't been done?

GOOD: The job hadn't been completed by the time she arrived back.

ROWAN: You've been around the Troubles long enough to realise the damage that had been done by the IRA's guns and explosives. So, that word "completion" you were talking about, the fact that here was a process that potentially was going to end all of that, must have given you some satisfaction.

GOOD: Oh, absolutely, and particularly when it came to the last day and the last item, that was a poignant moment. I'm not sure poignant is the right word, a pregnant moment, when all of us standing there at that moment would have had our own thoughts; the people from the IRA would have had their thoughts, the "decommissioners" would have had their thoughts because for them it was the completion of something that they had worked long and hard at for eight years...

ROWAN: This was the last item that Alex (Reid) talked about this week, the last rifle (being held by a member of the IRA)?

GOOD: This is right... I had my thoughts and found myself

saying, the kind of phrase we always say, whether we our
believers or not, Thank God, and I thought, I mean it, I do
mean it.

ROWAN: What about the days when you were with them, what
can you tell me about the days when you were with them – the
commissioners, the IRA, you and Alex? What sort of a week
was it?

GOOD: I can tell you this, that we were treated with respect,
respect for ourselves as persons, respect for our role and respect
for our independence both from the general and his colleagues
and from the representatives of the IRA who were there. I was
deeply conscious of that… I'm drawing a veil over any detail…
I think the detail is secondary, it's interesting, very interesting,
and there might come a time when I can give a little more
detail, but at the moment I am so conscious of the trust that
has been invested in me, and it may well be that others want to
invest trust in me for some other purpose or reason. So, I'm
most anxious to neither say nor do anything which could in
any way be construed as a betrayal of trust. Now, I've signed no
confidentiality clause – none of that. Nobody has asked me to
sign any confidentiality clause, nobody has even asked me
verbally to be totally confidential, but I respect the fact that
there is a confidentiality agreement between the general and his
colleagues and the IRA. I respect the reasons for that as well as
the agreement itself and I respect the way in which the general
and his colleagues have honoured that, and, therefore, I feel it
would be inappropriate for me to go down the road…

ROWAN: Of colouring in the picture.

GOOD: …colouring in the picture, because honour is something
which goes beyond what you write on paper, trust goes beyond
a contract, it is something that you know within yourself that
you must respect and honour, and as people respected me for
my role, I can do no less than respect what would be their
wishes. As far as the detail, I was saying, even if they

(journalists) ask us (Good and Reid): What did we have for breakfast, it sounds like a very innocent question, but before you know where you are, they're wanting to know: What kind of breakfast was it, and who cooked the breakfast? What sort of a building were you in when you were having your breakfast, and what time did you have your breakfast? And before you know where you are, you're starting to describe places and people and, unintentionally, in the most innocent way, unwittingly, you could be betraying trust, and, so, I felt it was not appropriate to go into the fine detail for all of those reasons, and, thirdly, they are all secondary to what this was all about. It is the outcome that is absolutely crucial.

ROWAN: In terms of that outcome, Harold, are you convinced that those weapons and the explosives that were put beyond use are in fact beyond use, that they cannot be retrieved – they cannot be used again by the IRA?

GOOD: I can see no way that they could ever be re-commissioned. The general is the person, who from a professional point of view, that's his job to make sure that they were decommissioned within the terms of the Decommissioning Act of 1997 which was agreed between the two governments.

ROWAN: Permanently unusable or permanently inaccessible.

GOOD: That they were destroyed within the terms of that. They were destroyed within the meaning of the Act, and I can with hand on heart testify that is what actually happened – took place. I have no hesitation in verifying that.

ROWAN: And one assumes that the place is a much safer place, having seen out of your eyes what you saw?

GOOD: One of the things that some people have said to us and it came up at this meeting the other night (at Fitzroy Presbyterian Church) was now these weapons have gone, evidence has gone with them. I can understand if I was in their shoes, I might well feel exactly the same. None of us know how we would feel unless we have been in that situation, but someone who has lost a loved one and for whom no one has ever been brought to account, feels that evidence has been destroyed along with the weapon; yeah, I can understand that, but there is a hard decision to be made there. In destroying the weapons you have destroyed the possibility of another victim.

ROWAN: Destroying the weapon, maybe saves a life?

GOOD: You save a life. Retaining it will not bring back the life of the lost loved one, but by destroying it you're destroying the possibility of it ever being used again on another person. And so you're hopefully ensuring the safety of other lives. So, those are the hard decisions that have to be made and those are the choices; the victims and their families, I can understand, but those are some of the hard choices, and I think if we were all given that choice, well, I would be surprised if people wouldn't say: Get rid of the stuff.

ROWAN: You talked about your last words from your wife when you left her, be careful, take care; what about her first words when you came back, or your first words to her?

GOOD: I think it was just like a loving reunion, and just good to be home, great to see you. I think it was just like a loving reunion, probably just like somebody who has been absent from home and returning home, and what you were up to and what you were at is really not that important.(It is) the fact that you are home safe and sound.

ROWAN: Let's go back to the word "completion" that she mentioned, were you able to tell her that you felt the job had been completed, that that part of our history was behind us?

GOOD: Oh yes, when we had a quiet moment to talk, I was able to say it was right to do it, you were right to support me in the doing of it. I thanked her for being so supportive and for being understanding and for what I know was a very stressful time for her while I was not here and she did not know where I was, and I think the huge, huge amount of appreciation that has come our way, huge amount, we had five negative communications;

at this moment, I can still count on one hand the negative communications by way of phone calls, email or letter, and there were five, and we have a file full of letters, my email is full, the telephone didn't stop for two or three days, which all confirmed the rightness of doing it... I had a letter from a policeman's daughter, whose father was injured, saying how grateful she was, a phone call from him as well... a whole range of people in the community, some who gave names, some who didn't, but who one way or the other, were saying this was a very important moment for them. And, again, I understand the misgivings. You can't have 35 years of murder and mayhem and pain and destruction without people having great difficulty... we all need space.

ROWAN: To absorb this.

GOOD: To absorb this. For some people it has been a shock. That's across the communities. There are republicans in shock as well as other people.

ROWAN: For different reasons.

GOOD: For different reasons, absolutely. And we have to give people space and we have to give people time, but we can't leave it too long because that would be to leave a further vacuum, which is not in any of our interests.

ROWAN: You are very conscious that this is one set of guns that have been dealt with. How hopeful are you, as a minister who served on the Shankill Road for many years, that the loyalists can take some encouragement from what has happened and maybe follow suit?

GOOD: I would be very careful not to say: "Right now boys, come on, this lot have handed in theirs, come on now, your turn." I don't think that would be a helpful way of approaching it – trying to put some kind of moral blackmail on people. It could be seen as that, but, obviously, we're longing, this community is longing for all who hold illegal weapons to make them available in whatever way they can agree with the international

body – the Independent International Decommissioning
Commission – whatever way they can do it; it would be my
hope that such people could begin, and I have reason to believe
that there are those out there who are thinking about this, and
I would encourage them to think well about that, because this
community needs the confidence that comes from knowing
that whatever debates we have, whatever difference we have, we
have the gun removed. The threat's no longer there from either
side… We would hope… that this could be a benchmark for
conflict situations around the world. I think this (the
decommissioning process) is unique; an undefeated group of
people who have made their weapons available for independent
decommissioning.

ROWAN: And not in a surrender sense.

GOOD: And not in a surrender sense.

ROWAN: You're totally satisfied Harold, that what you did was the
right thing to do and that the job is done?

GOOD: Absolutely. The question that people have asked and will
continue to ask (is): Are all the weapons gone? General de
Chastelain dealt with that question and dealt with it well on
the day of the event itself, and he was saying: Who knows?
Things can turn up, and may well turn up… As General de
Chastelain said there may well be things that are here or there,
but what we have said is, this is as we understand it the arsenal
of the IRA. And whatever credibility they have or do not have,
if this were not for real, their credibility would be gone
forever…

ROWAN: They've put their credibility more on the line than you've
put yours on the line?

GOOD: Absolutely. I've been asked all kinds of interesting
questions about putting yourself forward into this situation…
I said there is a great line in the scriptures where we are asked
to be fools for Christ's sake which in secular parlance means
being prepared to stick your neck out in the interests of the

greater good. I am prepared to, even if I were proved to be a fool, or if people thought me to be a fool, I don't think I will be proved to be a fool, but if people thought me to be a fool, for Christ's sake if it is something for the greater good. I've got twelve grandchildren. My children have never known what it is to live in a community at peace with itself. I would love to think that if there's anything I can leave my grandchildren, it will be some little part in the leaving of a community of people who are at peace with themselves and at peace with each other.

In this place, in this community, peace is a thing that has come dropping slow. It is not yet fully achieved. The IRA delivered on decommissioning, but not the kind of decommissioning that Paisley had demanded with the additional proof of photographs and with his preferred witness present. But all of that seems so irrelevant now. These were the arguments of yesterday; tomorrow is about something else. It was Gerry Adams who said to me on the day of the de Chastelain news conference in September – on that biggest day of decommissioning, that the job was done and that it couldn't be done twice. There will always be questions about how "total" it was. Indeed, I can remember a conversation with de Chastelain and his official Aaro Suonio when I told them I didn't believe there would ever be "complete" decommissioning. But Harold Good is right and so too is Peter Robinson. If any IRA guns were to surface and be used, then the credibility of that organisation would be gone forever, and the credibility of Adams and McGuinness would fall with it.

This process has moved into another phase now – a phase in which the players want to be certain that the IRA has gone. Only then might it be possible to think again of trying to build that once unthinkable deal between Paisley and the Provos. Much now depends on the reporting of the Independent Monitoring Commission – on the assessments that are given by its Commissioners, Lord Alderdice, Joe Brosnan, John Grieve and

Dick Kerr. They will report again in January of 2006, but to suggest that it would be possible then to give a definitive assessment on IRA future intentions would be to place that report on a very high pedestal indeed. It will take longer than that. We are dealing here with an organisation that is more than thirty five years old in this current phase of conflict, and, realistically, it will take more than thirty weeks to assess and make judgements on its future plans. Speaking to me for this book, the Secretary of State Peter Hain said he did not expect that negotiations would "be easy or absolutely instant", but he recognises the great distance the two sides – Paisley and Provos – have travelled towards making a deal, and at the same time he acknowledges that "the last few feet" will be the most difficult. The IRA did not want to give Paisley any part in the decommissioning process. That is why it rejected his demands for photographs and it is why it set its face against his choice of witness. On the other side of the coin, had a deal been done in December 2004, the DUP would not have put its hand up for Martin McGuinness in government. Another appointment mechanism was going to be used.

No one is saying that it is going to be easy. Indeed Paisley has likened a DUP-Sinn Féin government to "all hell being let loose". But, when he is asked about future possibilities, he is not saying "No" and he is not saying "Never", and that is what is different – that the once unthinkable is now being discussed in terms of the possible.

PAISLEY: I think that we have got to get it right now. If we don't get it right this time, well I would despair. I would honestly despair. I've never despaired, but, now, it's crucial that we get it right. And, at the end of the day, no one points and says: "Why did you not put your finger on that. Why did you not say: But what about that?" So I am trying to concentrate my mind now upon what we must have and cannot make peace or go into any peace process so-called, except the foundation is sound.

ROWAN: (Being sure) the IRA is away?

PAISLEY: Yes, the IRA is really away…

ROWAN: So, getting it right is your priority?

PAISLEY: Yes.

ROWAN: Getting the IRA away is your priority?

PAISLEY: Yes.

ROWAN: And if you can do those things, can there be a government with you and Sinn Féin – a very different Sinn Féin?

PAISLEY: It would be much like the Workers Party. It would be a complete and total change and that is not beyond us. It is not beyond us. But it is beyond us now as long as the IRA keeps on the way they're going. And I have never seen in all the talks really any real change. The IRA today is the same in its mentality as it was before they signed the Agreement and nobody has been converted…

ROWAN: I know you're saying it's difficult to see the circumstances (in which you would go into government with Sinn Féin), but you're not saying never?

PAISLEY: No, I'm a democrat and I believe the democratic way of life is right. But the democratic way of life must be the way of no guns, and no paramilitaries, no threats, no violence; a man is free to express himself, to get elected, to do his duty. He may love things that I hate.

ROWAN: But if that's democracy?

PAISLEY: That is democracy, freedom of expression, but I could not in any way have any making of any government in Northern Ireland that I'm asked to bring in people who have not given that (violence) up for all time and proved it. And I regret that the IRA have made some terrible statements really rejoicing and saying, "Look, we are saluting the memory of these men…"

ROWAN: You need the proof and you need to be convinced is what you're saying?

PAISLEY: That right, that's right, need absolute proof. So that we are not going to get… What would happen say that I went into government and the IRA did something again? (It would be said) 'You were a fool', and all that you did would be forgotten in five minutes. You're actually putting your future into the hands of the IRA. Well it's like asking me to put my soul into the hands of the devil, and I can only describe it that way… Any politician that's in the position I'm in, he must realise that if he's going to take decisions, which he'll have to take, he must be satisfied in his own mind, and if I was satisfied in my own mind about things, I would have the courage to do it.

Ian Paisley won't say it, but many others are thinking it – thinking there is now something inevitable about where this process will end up – that "where" being in a new power-sharing government at Stormont. And if that is the end point, then the DUP and Sinn Féin will have done political business, and, in any new Executive, they will be the lead parties. The IRA's statement of July 2005 and the subsequent acts of decommissioning may not have been all that the DUP wanted them to be, but that is politics. At the point of its ceasefire in 1994 and beyond the Good Friday Agreement, the IRA would not have envisaged Adams and McGuinness having to do business with Paisley. This process is what it is. The elections have delivered up new players – in terms of the main negotiators. It is now irrelevant that there were no photographs and that Paisley, with all his votes and all his political strength, was not able to get his way on the witness that he wanted. The chapter on IRA decommissioning is closed, and for the British Government and the Irish Government, the real significance of 2005 was the historical worth of an IRA statement ending its decades-long war.

That is why Blair and his government and the police and the Army responded so quickly to consolidate what had been achieved. That is why the Army is going and "Operation Banner" is ending.

We may have to wait a little longer for the politics of a power-sharing government to function again – but this process is now pointed in one direction only.

PETER ROBINSON: The government has this continuing concern about what the IRA might do in GB. They wanted to get them (the IRA) over the line on those issues (activities and decommissioning). They probably reckoned that a lot of the components of the deal (December '04 comprehensive agreement) that would satisfy Sinn Féin, they could deliver on their own, and therefore they did it by way of a two-way deal. At no stage did they consult us about what they were doing. They made, in my view, massive mistakes – errors – in the way they handled it. The comprehensive agreement may have included some of the aspects of decommissioning and so forth, but in every element of it they got it wrong. They bowled short in terms of witnesses. They bowled short in terms of photographs. The government, when they weren't having their backbone strengthened for them, just caved in on all of those issues, so enthusiastic were they to get the IRA's guns. They made a series of concessions in order to get it, but didn't have the commonsense to recognise that if they simply did concessions on one side that it was having an impact on the other side. And the end result was that the whole of the unionist community just saw a series of concessions. Then what the IRA was doing was in exchange for it. Whereas on the comprehensive agreement there would have been confidence-building measures on the other side, they were absent in these circumstances and indeed the handling of the concessions that they gave to the IRA was appalling as well.

MARTIN McGUINNESS: Now that the issue of arms has been dealt with – the big issue that Ian Paisley majored on – at some stage Ian Paisley is going to have to come to his senses and recognise that the best thing to do is to conclude the deal that he should have concluded in December of last year.

ROWAN: Do you think the IRA's words and actions make more inevitable now that DUP-Sinn Féin deal – however long it takes?

McGUINNESS: Well, it makes it more likely. The big quandary I have, and I think that we just have to live with this, is that we are dealing with a particular unique personality that is Ian Paisley. What I'm trying to do, and what we're trying to do with him in the leadership of Sinn Féin is to bring about circumstances which will see Ian Paisley take a decision that many people thought he would never take.

ROWAN: Do the unthinkable?

McGUINNESS: Do the unthinkable from a unionist perspective, go into government with Sinn Féin, sit in an all-Ireland Ministerial Council and work constructively with the rest of us to build a better future for all of our people.

As Sinn Féin waits for Paisley, the political process is jogging on the spot. The peace process is not. What the IRA said and did in 2005 made it a very different organisation, and it made where we live a very different place. The Army clearly trusts what the IRA has said – and that means the police do as well. Decisions on demilitarisation or normalisation have to be approved by the Chief Constable who has operational responsibility for these matters. The watchtowers are coming off the hills in south Armagh, soldiers are leaving or retreating to barracks and the Royal Irish Regiment is to be stood down. In less than two years Operation Banner will have ended. So, what we are seeing is a battlefield of thirty-five years and more beginning to be cleared.

But, inside the world of loyalism, we are looking at an unpredictable situation. Here, sometimes, guns can be drawn more quickly than they are in a Wild West movie. But after the madness of the violence attached to that September march in west

Belfast, things began to settle in the loyalist community. Some in the paramilitary leadership began to think more clearly about what the IRA had said and done. And, now, the UVF is discussing with its membership the possibility of a dialogue with republicans – a dialogue with the "enemy". And what does that tell us? It tells us that the men of war on that side of the fence are beginning to think seriously about how they make peace on the other side of the fence. There will be more tremors in our world of politics and peace and sometimes violence. On-the-run suspects have still to come home. The vexed issue of policing has to be settled. And the politics of power-sharing have to work again. Will Paisley and the DUP do business or do a deal with republicans, with Adams and McGuinness? I am convinced they will. Just don't ask me precisely when and don't ask me exactly how.

An Address to the IRA by
Sinn Féin President Gerry Adams, April 6, 2005

I want to speak directly to the men and women of Oglaigh na hEireann, the volunteer soldiers of the Irish Republican Army.

In time of great peril you stepped into the Bearna Baoil, the gap of danger. When others stood idly by, you and your families gave your all, in defence of a risen people and in pursuit of Irish freedom and unity.

Against mighty odds you held the line and faced down a huge military foe, the British crown forces and their surrogates in the unionist death squads.

Eleven years ago the Army leadership ordered a complete cessation of military operations. This courageous decision was in response to proposals put forward by the Sinn Féin leadership to construct a peace process, build democratic politics and achieve a lasting peace.

Since then, despite many provocations and setbacks, the cessation has endured.

And more than that, when elements within the British and Irish establishments and rejectionist unionism delayed progress, it was the IRA leadership which authorised a number of significant initiatives to enhance the peace process.

On a number of occasions commitments have been reneged on. These include commitments from the two governments.

The Irish Republican Army has kept every commitment made by its leadership.

The most recent of these was last December when the IRA was

prepared to support a comprehensive agreement. At that time the Army leadership said the implementation of this agreement would allow everyone, including the IRA, to take its political objectives forward by peaceful and democratic means.

That agreement perished on the rock of unionist intransigence. The shortsightedness of the two governments compounded the difficulties.

Since then there has been a vicious campaign of vilification against republicans, driven in main by the Irish government. There are a number of reasons for this.

The growing political influence of Sinn Féin is a primary factor.

The unionists also for their part, want to minimise the potential for change, not only on the equality agenda but on the issues of sovereignty and ending the union.

The IRA is being used as the excuse by them all not to engage properly in the process of building peace with justice in Ireland.

For over thirty years the IRA showed that the British government could not rule Ireland on its own terms. You asserted the legitimacy of the right of the people of this island to freedom and independence. Many of your comrades made the ultimate sacrifice.

Your determination, selflessness and courage have brought the freedom struggle towards its fulfilment.

That struggle can now be taken forward by other means. I say this with the authority of my office as President of Sinn Féin.

In the past I have defended the right of the IRA to engage in armed struggle. I did so because there was no alternative for those who would not bend the knee, or turn a blind eye to oppression, or for those who wanted a national republic.

Now there is an alternative.

I have clearly set out my view of what that alternative is. The way forward is by building political support for republican and democratic objectives across Ireland and by winning support for these goals internationally.

I want to use this occasion therefore to appeal to the leadership of Oglaigh na hEireann to fully embrace and accept this alternative.

Can you take courageous initiatives which will achieve your aims by purely political and democratic activity?

I know full well that such historic decisions can only be taken in the aftermath of intense internal consultation. I ask that you initiate this as quickly as possible.

I understand fully that the IRA's most recent positive contribution to the peace process was in the context of a comprehensive agreement. But I also hold the very strong view that republicans need to lead by example.

There is no greater demonstration of this than the IRA cessation in the summer of 1994.

Sinn Féin has demonstrated the ability to play a leadership role as part of a popular movement towards peace, equality and justice.

We are totally committed to ending partition and to creating the conditions for unity and independence. Sinn Féin has the potential and capacity to become the vehicle for the attainment of republican objectives.

The Ireland we live in today is also a very different place from 15 years ago. There is now an all-Ireland agenda with huge potential.

Nationalists and republicans have a confidence that will never again allow anyone to be treated as second class citizens. Equality is our watchword.

The catalyst for much of this change is the growing support for republicanism.

Of course, those who oppose change are not going to simply roll over. It will always be a battle a day between those who want maximum change and those who want to maintain the status quo. But if republicans are to prevail, if the peace process is to be successfully concluded and Irish sovereignty and re-unification secured, then we have to set the agenda – no one else is going to do that.

So, I also want to make a personal appeal to all of you – the women and men volunteers who have remained undefeated in the face of tremendous odds.

Now is the time for you to step into the Bearna Baoil again; not as volunteers risking life and limb but as activists in a national movement towards independence and unity.

Such decisions will be far-reaching and difficult. But you never lacked courage in the past. Your courage is now needed for the future.

It won't be easy. There are many problems to be resolved by the people of Ireland in the time ahead. Your ability as republican volunteers, to rise to this challenge will mean that the two governments and others cannot easily hide from their obligations and their responsibility to resolve these problems.

Our struggle has reached a defining moment.

I am asking you to join me in seizing this moment, to intensify our efforts, to rebuild the peace process and decisively move our struggle forward.

The leadership of Oglaigh na hEireann has formally ordered an end to the armed campaign. This will take effect from 4.00pm this afternoon.

All IRA units have been ordered to dump arms.

All Volunteers have been instructed to assist the development of purely political and democratic programmes through exclusively peaceful means. Volunteers must not engage in any other activities whatsoever.

The IRA leadership has also authorised our representative to engage with the IICD to complete the process to verifiably put its arms beyond use in a way which will further enhance public confidence and to conclude this as quickly as possible. We have invited two independent witnesses, from the Protestant and Catholic churches, to testify to this.

The Army Council took these decisions following an unprecedented internal discussion and consultation process with IRA units and Volunteers.

We appreciate the honest and forthright way in which the consultation process was carried out and the depth and content of the submissions. We are proud of the comradely way in which this truly historic discussion was conducted.

The outcome of our consultations show very strong support among IRA Volunteers for the Sinn Féin peace strategy. There is also widespread concern about the failure of the two governments and the unionists to fully engage in the peace process. This has created real difficulties. The overwhelming majority of people in

Ireland fully support this process. They and friends of Irish unity throughout the world want to see the full implementation of the Good Friday Agreement.

Notwithstanding these difficulties our decisions have been taken to advance our republican and democratic objectives, including our goal of a united Ireland. We believe there is now an alternative way to achieve this and to end British rule in our country.

It is the responsibility of all Volunteers to show leadership, determination and courage. We are very mindful of the sacrifices of our patriot dead, those who went to jail, Volunteers, their families and the wider republican base. We reiterate our view that the armed struggle was entirely legitimate.

We are conscious that many people suffered in the conflict. There is a compelling imperative on all sides to build a just and lasting peace.

The issue of the defence of nationalist and republican communities has been raised with us. There is a responsibility on society to ensure that there is no re-occurance of the pogroms of 1969 and the early 1970s. There is also a universal responsibility to tackle sectarianism in all its forms.

The IRA is fully committed to the goals of Irish unity and independence and to building the republic outlined in the 1916 Proclamation.

We call for maximum unity and effort by Irish republicans everywhere. We are confident that by working together Irish republicans can achieve our objectives. Every Volunteer is aware of the import of the decisions we have taken and all Oglaigh are compelled to fully comply with these orders.

There is now an unprecedented opportunity to utilise the considerable energy and goodwill which there is for the peace process. This comprehensive series of unparalleled initiatives is our contribution to this and to the continued endeavours to bring about independence and unity for the people of Ireland.

P O'Neill

APPENDIX 3

Report of the Independent Internal Commission
on Decommissioning, September 26, 2005

To:

The Rt Hon Peter Hain, MP
Secretary of State for
  Northern Ireland
BELFAST

To:

Mr Michael McDowell, TD
Minister for Justice, Equality
  and Law Reform
DUBLIN

1. Over the past number of weeks we have engaged with the IRA representative in the execution of our mandate to decommission paramilitary arms.

2. We can now report that we have observed and verified events to put beyond use very large quantities of arms which the representative has informed us includes all the arms in the IRA's possession. We have made an inventory of this *materiel*.

3. In 2004 the Commission was provided with estimates of the number and quantity of arms held by the IRA. These estimates were produced by the security forces in both jurisdictions and were in agreement. Our inventory is consistent with these estimates and we believe that the arms decommissioned represent the totality of the IRA's arsenal.

4. The manner in which the arms were decommissioned is in

accordance with the remit given us by the two governments as reflected in their Decommissioning Acts of 1997.

5. A Protestant and a Catholic clergyman also witnessed all these recent events: the Reverend Harold Good, former President of the Methodist Church in Ireland, and Father Alec Reid, a Redemptorist priest.

6. The new single inventory of decommissioned IRA arms incorporates the three we made during the preceding IRA events. This lists all the IRA arms we have verified as having been put beyond use. We will retain possession of this inventory until our mandate is complete.

7. We can report, however, that the arms involved in the recent events include a full range of ammunition, rifles, machine guns, mortars, missiles, handguns, explosives, explosive substances and other arms, including all the categories described in the estimates provided by the security forces.

8. In summary, we have determined that the IRA has met its commitment to put all its arms beyond use in a manner called for by legislation.

9. It remains for us to address the arms of the loyalist paramilitary groups, as well as other paramilitary organizations, when these are prepared to cooperate with us in doing so.

Tauno Nieminen　　　*John de Chastelain*　　　*Andrew Sens*
26 September 2005

APPENDIX 4

IRA Statement, September 26, 2005

The leadership of Oglaigh na hEireann announced on July 28th that we had authorised our representative to engage with the IICD to complete the process to verifiably put arms beyond use. The IRA leadership can now confirm that the process of putting our arms beyond use has been completed.

P O'Neill

APPENDIX 5

LVF Statement, October 30, 2005

The leadership of the LVF have today ordered all their military units to stand down. This decision is taken as a direct response to recent IRA actions and statements. While we remain sceptical about their intent to desist permanently from violence we believe there is sufficient evidence to allow for the exploration for peaceful co-existence within Northern Ireland, following the significant amount of IRA ordnance which has been destroyed recently indicating that in the foreseeable future the threat of a renewed IRA campaign is unlikely. After an extensive consultation with community and church leaders, the LVF has taken this positive step in the best interest of loyalism, which will be served in the future by a political and community response rather than a military one. Over recent years the confidence of loyalist communities has been weakened by internal feuding indulged in by all as well as criminality, which has dishonoured the memory of all our fallen comrades. Due to the recent two month cessation of violence in relation to feuding, the LVF has been able to continue with their internal discussions and have decided to lead the way by leaving the stage not from a position of weakness or under threat. Our volunteers and leadership know their capabilities, but in the interests of loyalism where we lead we hope others will follow. We salute all our fallen comrades and pay tribute to our volunteers, families and friends who have supported their loved ones over the years. Lead the way.